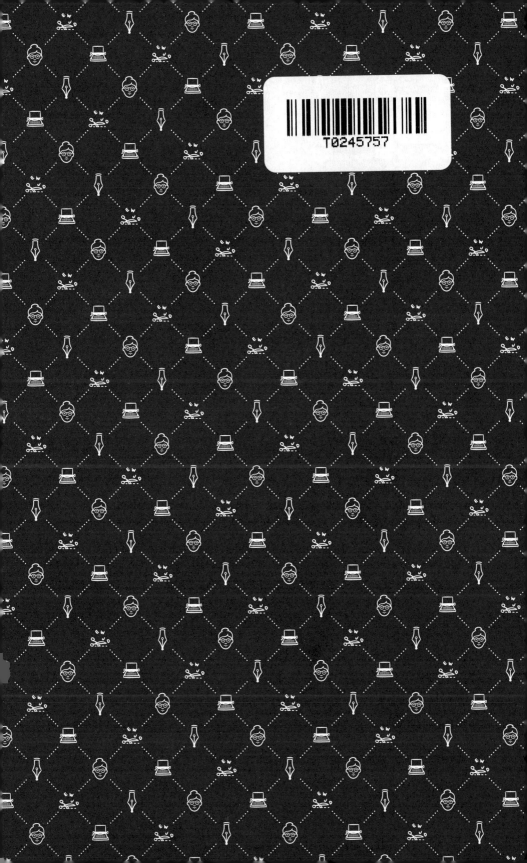

Storyville!

Also by John Dufresne

Storyville!

An Illustrated Guide to Writing Fiction

John Dufresne

Illustrated by Evan Wondolowski

W. W. NORTON & COMPANY
Independent Publishers Since 1923

For information about permission to reproduce selections from this book, write to
Permissions, W. W. Norton & Company, Inc., 500 Fifth Avenue, New York, NY 10110

For information about special discounts for bulk purchases, please contact
W. W. Norton Special Sales at specialsales@wwnorton.com or 800-233-4830

Manufacturing by Versa Press
Production manager: Beth Steidle

ISBN 978-0-393-60840-3

W. W. Norton & Company, Inc., 500 Fifth Avenue, New York, N.Y. 10110
www.wwnorton.com

W. W. Norton & Company Ltd., 15 Carlisle Street, London W1D 3BS

1 2 3 4 5 6 7 8 9 0

What thou seest, write in a book . . .

Acknowledgments

We want to thank Jill Bialosky, who, as always, helped make this a better book than it would have been. And thanks to our agent Bill Clegg for his efforts on behalf of *Storyville*. To Drew Weitman, our extraordinary assistant editor, and to Dave Cole, friend and copy editor. And to all the writers in our Movable Writing Feast: Teddy and Jim Bob Jones, Kim Bradley, Cully and Susan Perlman, Karen and Garry Kravit, Jill Coupe, Scott and Sandy Jones, Peter Stravlo and Peggy McGivern, David and Rosie Norman, Liz Trupin-Pulli, Jean Dowdy, Kim Bradley, Jim Herod, Maureen Welch and Sherry Dickerson, Jose Sary, Bruce Harvey, Connie St. Clair, Melanie Mochan, Stephanie Josie, Frances Nevill, Joy Dickinson, Sally Bowditch, Gail Randall, Karin Cadora, Liz Ferrer, John Green, Robert Miller, Jeff Williams, Sandi Hutcheson, Helena Rho, Cheryl Romo, Joan Baker, Margaret Mooney, Susan Lolis, Chervis Isom, Annelle Gordon, Jim Cowart, Charlyn Rainville, Mike Oldham, Karen Herzog, Nancy Palmer, Michael Sheriff, Mo Donnelly, Kelly Canaday, Susan Brandt, Dwan Tape, to all the folks at Sundog Books in Seaside and Books & Books in Miami, to the Friday Night Writers, and to John's office mate and BFF, Theodore Harrison-Rowan, who sat down one morning and wrote this poem:

park

I went to the park with my friend Lola. We played for a long time. I was Lola's friend since I was three when I met Lola; now Lola is eight and I am always a year younger than Lola. Now I am seven years old.

GROUPS

We played in groups. Lola went with just girls I went with just boys; we played soccer, tennis, and hide in seek. The girls were the ages between eight—ten years old, and mine were teens.

AT HOME

Lastly, we played in my room or the house. We were still friends. We had a few snacks (two is a few); we ate chetoes and fruit roll-ups THE END

Storyville!

Chapter One

The Fiction Writer

A writer never has a vacation. For a writer, life consists of either writing or thinking about writing.

—Eugene Ionesco

Introduction

You need at least two skills to be a fiction writer. You have to be able to write and you have to be able to tell a story. Telling a story is the harder skill to master.

My dear friend Charlie Willig was the most fascinating storyteller I ever met. And he was full of stories. He could keep you engrossed all day long. He could tell you about laying a pipeline in Oklahoma and keep you riveted to your chair and laughing to beat the band. He knew stories about everyone we worked with, everyone in Augusta, Georgia, it seemed. I'd say, Charlie, you need to write these down. But he never did. Turns out I was wrong. He didn't need to write them down. He just needed to tell them. He liked the intimacy and the immediacy of the auditor's response, which is something writers have to do without. He liked an audience. The audience, often an audience of one, brought out the scamp in Charlie. I wanted him to come on by every morning to the rent house he found for us, and tell me a story or two—give me something to spend the day writing about. And he knew how to tell a story. He did not rush. He painted pictures. I couldn't figure out how so many interesting and funny things were happening to Charlie. Years later I read something that Allan Gurganis wrote about stories: "Know something, sugar? Stories only happen to the people who can tell them." That was Charlie's secret.

When I remember Charlie's storytelling skills I am reminded of Chekhov's sledge driver Iona Potapov in the story "Misery," who needs to tell the story of his dead son: "His son will soon have been dead a week, and he has not really talked to anybody yet. . . . He wants to talk of it properly, with deliberation. . . . He wants to tell how his son was taken ill, how he suffered, what he said before he died, how he died. . . . He wants to describe the funeral, and how he went to the hospital to get his son's clothes. He still has his daughter Anisya in the country. . . . And he wants to talk about her too. . . . Yes, he has plenty to talk about now. His listener ought to sigh and exclaim and lament. . . ."

To whom shall I tell my grief?

We read stories and write them to make sense of our lives, to be entertained, and to feel something. We read and write and tell them to be transported to another, more lucid and compelling world, to learn about ourselves and about what it's like to be a human being. This narrative impulse is as basic as breathing. Children understand stories before they understand math or anything else. They want stories, and as soon as they can speak, they tell stories. We are *Homo fabulator*—man the storyteller—and that may be all that separates us from the other creatures on this earth.

We can, and we did, do without writing for thousands of years. But we have never done without stories.

There have been great societies that did not use the wheel, but there have been no societies that did not tell stories.

–Ursula K. Le Guin

Man is eminently a storyteller. His search for a purpose, a cause, an ideal, a mission and the like is largely a search for a plot and a pattern in the development of his life story – a story that is basically without meaning or pattern.

–Eric Hoffer

All the technology you'll ever need to kick-start your fiction-writing career:

 A flat surface. A table, a desk, a lapboard. If you're tall, you can stand and use the top of the fridge as six-foot-six inch Thomas Wolfe did. Otherwise, you'll want a chair. The flat surface might be a thick book on your lap as you lie in bed. Nabokov wrote like that with a pen and index cards. So, really, you don't even need a chair.

 A fountain pen and a bottle of ink. Or a ballpoint or a Sharpie. Or a pencil and a pencil sharpener. Stylus. (James Joyce wrote lying on his bed wearing a white coat. He wrote with crayons on cardboard—his vision, you see, was that impaired.) Or a computer of some kind and a plug.

 Paper or screen.

You can write at home. Or you can write outside the house. Every café and restaurant has tables, the flat surfaces we need. Every waiter has a pen we can borrow and a napkin we can write on. And all of those interesting people keep walking through the door and sitting near us. Our job as fiction writers is to eavesdrop on the people talking in public and to imagine the lives they lead when they leave the café. Write wherever you are!

 Don't have a napkin?
Write on your hand!

You can't want to be a writer.
You have to be writing.

Don't write fiction . . .

 If you don't know the basics of grammar and usage and syntax or are not willing to learn. Buy a stylebook (*The Chicago Manual of Style* is the industry standard, but there are many), study it, keep it by your desk. Spelling is important. So is punctuation. So are grammar and mechanics.

 If you think that ideas are more important than people or if you think the author is more important than his characters, his images, his lines.

 If you believe in the magic and divinity of spontaneous writing as final product. First thought is never best thought. All writing is rewriting. As first draft, spontaneous composition is desirable. But only then.

 If writing is primarily a way for you to get in touch with your feelings and to work out your problems. Writing is a wonderful tool for self-awareness, but that aspect is not our concern here. One of the first rules that the fiction writer must learn is that the reader does not care about her. The reader says tell me about me.

 If you haven't read a novel or a collection of stories in the last month. Why would you want to write something that you are not interested in reading?

 If you think that writing is the expression of a truth that you are privy to, if you have a message to deliver, in other words, to the insensitive reader, write an essay or a political tract or a manifesto. Fiction doesn't preach, it explores.

Write as much as you can! Write, write, write till your fingers break.

—Anton Chekhov

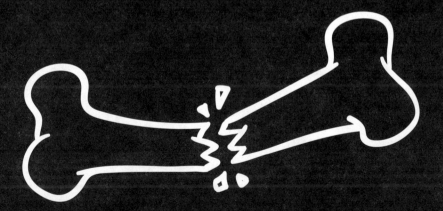

Our writing equipment takes part in the forming of our thoughts.

—Friedrich Nietzsche

The write stuff

So here's a question I'm often asked at writers' conferences and in writing workshops. Do you write with a pen or on the computer? This strikes me as an important and incisive question, though I've heard it disparaged by some as being naïve and irrelevant. But this is just the sort of guileless inquiry that I posed to the occasional visiting writer at my college (or more often wished to pose, because I was shy and crippled with doubt and anxiety) back when I was a reader and not a writer. There were no writers in my neighborhood, after all, so how else was I supposed to learn to do it? I was trying to imagine how writers did what they did. If I could visualize the creative process taking place, I thought, then maybe I could do it myself.

Some of us write with pens, some with pencils. Some may even insist on a particular brand of pencil, like John Steinbeck, who used a Blackwing 602, and wrote in his essay "The Art of Fiction": "I have found a new kind of pencil—the best I have ever had. Of course it costs three times as much too but it is black and soft but doesn't break off. I think I will always use these. They are called Blackwings and they really glide over the paper." Vladimir Nabokov wrote the screenplay for *Lolita*, by the way, with a Blackwing on a thousand index cards. Others of us compose on computers.

And some of us still crank out stories on a typewriter. (The venerable and commanding William Trevor worked on one or another of his four Olympia typewriters. He liked to hear the clacking sound of the typewriter as he worked, he said. John Updike used an Olivetti from the forties and later an Olympia Electric 65C, which sold at auction for $4,375 after his death. Hunter Thompson famously shot his cranky red IBM Selectric. Cormac McCarthy's battered Lettera 32 sold for $254,500 on eBay.)

When I learned from movies that writers typed their stories, often while smoking pipes, I was crestfallen. I thought I could never be a writer in that case because I couldn't type. (A little knowledge is such a dangerous thing.) And even though I was smoking cigarettes after Little League games, I knew the whole pipe business was a greater affectation than I could ever pull off. Meanwhile, as I busily scribble on my pages and order bottles of blue-black Quink online, young Japanese writers are punching out their novels on cell phones. The practice is called keitai shousetsu.

These thumb-novels are as minimalist as one might expect from the small-screen technology. Like this, we might imagine: "Once upon a time, and so on." Or, "A screaming came across the sky. The end." Well, maybe not that minimalist. The Japanese keitai shousetsu has evolved into the movella, which originated in Denmark and has spread, like swine flu, across the globe. These novels are published online, one chapter at a time. Most of the writers and readers are between thirteen and twenty. Justin Bieber often rides to the heroine's rescue in these novels, and vampires stalk the pages. Not a lot of attention is paid to grammar, punctuation, mechanics, or usage. LOL. Emoticons, on the other hand, are a frequent shorthand. And the movella might also include handy hyperlinks to, say, beauty products mentioned in the story. The author might humbly apologize in the comment section for a boring chapter but promise excitement ahead and will let you know who she sees playing her characters' roles in the inevitable movie.

So where were we? Ah, yes, writing instruments! I happen to write with a fountain pen (I have dozens) because I like going slow on white, never yellow, paper (Trevor used blue, by the way, as did Friedrich Schiller), a white, lined 8½" × 11" tablet, with two columns, the narrower left-hand column for annotations, and an unlined box across the bottom of the page labeled "task list" for more notes. I write many drafts longhand. I change sentences, words, and phrases as I write, often recopying the entire annotated draft from the first line to the point at which the corrections get so messy and confusing that I have to stop and make a fresh copy. And in this way I get to feel the rhythm of the prose, hear the tone and the music of the narrative voice. As a result, the first lines of my stories and chapters are rewritten more than the last lines. Each draft, each rewritten page, is neater and more competent than the previous one. I find that I even sabotage myself by deliberately misspelling a word, so I'll have to rewrite the page again. I know that each time I undermine my tendency to be lazy in this way, the story improves. (I need to get less anal about it all because I have many stories I want to write, and have decidedly less time to write them in. I'm writing against the clock—we all are.) However we do the writing, we do it every day. Because we might delay, but time will not.

When I'm finally satisfied that the elements of plot are somewhat in place, and I think that at last I know what my characters want and why they want it, I type this draft into the computer. I print it out, then put the copy away for a few days, few weeks, as long as I can. And I work on another story. When I read the draft again with the freshness of vision that time has presented me, I immediately begin to tear it apart with great satisfaction.

Writers eventually find the composing process that works for them and stick with it. Or they keep experimenting to find an even more propitious process. And they also experiment with their writing time. Some of us write in the morning, some late at night. Some of us have to sneak in minutes here and there from our hectic and disordered days. Some of us write in noisy restaurants, some in cozy offices. Some of those offices are windowless, some are open to the world. Dame Edith Sitwell sometimes wrote lying down in an open coffin. Some of us write in silence. Some of us put on music. (But only if the music is without lyrics, in my case.) Some of us shut out the world; others of us can be interrupted. Most of us write wherever we are, meaning we take along a notebook, a memo pad, a laptop, or an iPad, and we jot down lines that might make their way to our story. Write at the desk, at the kitchen table, on the bus, in the coffee shop, in bed, and while driving, but remember to save those compound-complex sentences for the red lights.

Long answer short. As I said earlier, if you have a pencil and a piece of paper, you have the tools you need. Now you have to learn to use them. You do that by sitting down at the writing desk and using them day after day. Thinking about writing is not writing. Planning to write is not writing. Telling your friends you're a writer is not writing.

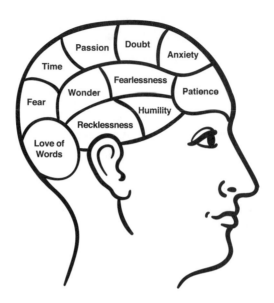

What you'll need to bring to the writing table:

A sense of wonder

An assertive curiosity about the world and the people who live in it. To this end, what you don't know is more important than what you know. (Which is good news for most of us.) You don't have to be smart to write fiction, but you do have to be curious.

Humility

You're not as smart as you thought you were. Fiction teaches you that real quick. The story in your head isn't breathing on the page. How come? And as I've said, no one cares about the author. We only care about the characters in the story. If you're writing for your ego, write a column in the *Penny Saver*, and they'll put your headshot in every issue.

Patience

Writing a story wasn't built in a day. Think of patience as persistence, as grace under duress. Think of patience as genius. Consider Tobias Wolff's words: "We are made to persist. That's how we find out who we are."

Fear

Afraid to fail at something you think is so important and transformative? Well, get used to it. All art is a failure. Here's Nobel Laureate Samuel Beckett: "Ever tried. Ever failed. No matter. Try again. Fail again. Fail better."

Love of words

Their sense and the music they make. Words are all we have. But they are enough. There are 600,000 words in the second edition of *The Oxford English Dictionary*. According to the Global Language Monitor, there are 1,052,010.5 words in the English language as of January 1, 2019. But we don't have a word for the feeling of longing for something or someone we love that is lost (but the Brazilians do: *saudade*). Yes, we may call some words synonyms, but no two words mean exactly the same thing.

Doubt and anxiety

If this were easy, everyone would be doing it. Don't go to therapy for anxiety. Bring the anxiety to the page where it'll do you and your characters some good. A therapist's job is to help you tell your story. Writing a story will serve the same purpose.

Passion

It can't be taught. It's a strong or overpowering need, an excitement to write and to tell stories. You have to love the process of making meaning and shaping chaos into coherence.

Fearlessness

You may not be able to overcome your fears (of the blank page, of the unknown, of failure, of solitude, of rejection, of inadequacy, of vulnerability, of giving up, of criticism, of exposure, of offending, of being read, of not being read) but you can learn to live with them.

Time, time, time

In short supply for all of us. And there is less of it now than there was this morning. What you don't write today will never get written.

A certain recklessness

You have to want to take some risks. A glorious failure is, perhaps, more of a triumph than a timid success. After all, every novel has something wrong with it, as Randall Jarrell said. And a certain strangeness would also help.

What is a notebook?

+ It's an anthology, not a diary (and not a journal, necessarily). It's about what's out there in the world.

+ It's a tool, not an obsession.

+ It's about stimulation, not facts.

+ It's about what could happen, not what did happen.

+ It's a mess, not a lesson plan or guidebook.

+ It's a warehouse, not a museum.

+ It's a means, not an end.

+ First you gather and collect, then you sort and apply.

+ It's for your eyes only, not for publication.

Why keep a notebook?

+ As a reminder that you're a writer.

+ You see differently with a pen in your hand.

+ You think differently with a notebook open in front of you.

+ It helps you to pay attention to the world and to your own thoughts.

+ It encourages you to write.

+ Serves notice to the world: "I'm a writer!"

+ It's a magnet for your stories.

+ It keeps the creative juices flowing.

+ It preserves what would be forgotten (a memory bank).

+ It affords you the opportunity to write when you have only five minutes.

+ Writing engenders more writing.

+ It's a repository of material that you will mine.

Note-taking is a creative act. You make a note about a woman's blouse. Then you wonder where she lives, and you see her apartment, and you can tell she lives alone but has a cat, and the cat's a marbled tabby named Cochise. Then you wonder what her job is. And so it goes . . .

Try to be one of those people on whom nothing is lost.

—Henry James

Imagination is more important than knowledge.

–Albert Einstein

What's kept in a notebook?

 Remarks overheard in the line at the Wells Fargo Bank: "Where would I be if I were a straw?"

 Eavesdropped conversations: like the one you heard at Wan's about the boss with a brain tumor who is firing a woman he's been sleeping with.

 Magazine and newspaper articles: "Mummified woman thought she'd come back to life"; "New Mexico man set on fire after losing bet."

 Photos: of your cat, Cochise.

 Phrases: "American owned." In the South this is code for, "This motel is not owned by a Pakistani."

 Words you like: *scoon*—to skip across the water like a stone; *Ken-Taco-Hut*.

 Images: a walker with tennis balls on the rear legs.

 Names: Asbestos Felt; Achy Obejas; Crickett Abbott; Toochis Morin. All seen on movie credits—a wonderful place to find unusual names.

 Writing exercises: Write twenty-five sentences that begin with "I remember . . ."

 Found poems (this from an obit): "She enjoyed shopping, doing crossword puzzles, cooking, popping bubble wrap, and collecting angels."

 Words about writing: About the old saw "Write what you know," Auden said, "But you don't know what you know until you write it."

Lines that intrigue: "The point of life is to fail at greater and greater things." Rilke.

In short—anything at all!

By making a note of something that strikes you, you separate it from the incessant stream of impressions that crowd across the mental eye, and perhaps fix it in your memory. All of us have had good ideas or vivid sensations that we thought would one day come in useful, but which, because we were too lazy to write them down, have entirely escaped us. When you know you are going to make a note of something, you look at it more attentively than you otherwise would, and in the process of doing so the words are borne in upon you that will give it its private place in reality.
—W. SOMERSET MAUGHAM

Insights don't usually arrive at my desk, but go into notebooks when I'm on the move. Or half-asleep.

—Hilary Mantel

Speak, memory!

Explore your life, your values, and your emotions as a source of material for stories. Flannery O'Connor said that anyone who has survived beyond the age of twelve has enough fictional material for the rest of her life. And remember, too, the unexamined life is not worth living. Write the answers in that notebook you bought!

 What are your tastes in music, books, painting, sports, cars, foods, beverages, films, plants, furniture, houses, politicians, magazines, appliances, friends, TV shows? Have your tastes changed as you've grown? If so, how? And why?

 Describe what you remember of your childhood prior to beginning school. Do you remember your toys, your dolls, your room? Where did you play when you played outside? What is your earliest memory? Your first memory is where you say your life begins.

 Discuss three events that have caused you to be profoundly unhappy. And it's not always the obvious events that make us the saddest. Think hard. What is the best thing that has happened to you in your life? The worst?

 What are your major fears? We think of phobias as abnormal and irrational, but they still count. And not all fears are irrational. Give examples of your fears and try to trace the fears back to childhood incidents if you can. Maybe you're afraid of the dark for a good reason.

 When do you feel most at ease and comfortable? And where? And what are you doing when you are at this ease? Are you alone?

How do you think you'll die? How would you *like* to die? *Like*, I suppose, is the wrong word. Imagine your own funeral, your wake, the gathering after the burial. (This is your only chance to be there.) What are they saying about you?

What are your attitudes toward the opposite sex, love, money, insanity, suicide, abortion, violence, family life, animals, poverty? Remember that our attitudes are seldom simple, often ambivalent. Be honest with yourself. Maybe you're a liberal and a feminist and believe in a woman's right to choose, but you're not sure what you'd do if you were confronted with an unwanted pregnancy.

What would you like to change about yourself? Why haven't you done it already? When will you start the change?

What are the motivating forces in your life? What are your ambitions? Describe your life in ten years as you want it to be. How would you live if you could have anything you want? What do you want?

Describe any jobs you've had. Talk about the people you worked with.

Have you had any mystical experiences? What were they? How does it feel like to talk about them?

What did you want to be when you were five? When you were ten? Why aren't you that person you dreamed of being? Do you still long to be that person? What's stopping you?

Remember the worst part of being a child. Dramatize it. Remember the best of it and dramatize that.

Write about all of the places you have ever lived. Describe each house in great and loving detail. Recall if you were happy or unhappy in these places and why. Describe the kitchens, the yards, your bedrooms, the neighbors, the views, etc. What were the family dynamics in each house? List the smells that you remember and the memories they conjure. Remember the meals.

What are your regrets? How does it feel to write about your life? Write about the emotions you feel as you remember and as you write.

Imagination, Provocation, and Susceptibility

W. H. Auden said the first act of writing is noticing. Noticing begins with a sense of wonder, an assertive curiosity about the world, a wanting to know how and why. Your job as a writer is to see what no one else sees, to see what's there, not what's supposed to be there, or to see what others see but think about it differently. You savor what others dismiss. You know that an image or idea on its own might be static, but combined with another can become dynamic, can resonate and illuminate. Emerson said, "In every work of genius, we recognize our own rejected thoughts . . . " And because you can't know which images will respond to stimulation, you collect them all. Someday, you trust, you will use them.

It's a provocative world out there, and you try to make yourself susceptible to it. You understand that every object is worthy of your attention because a story can begin anywhere, because everything is implicit in anything, because any irritating grain of sand can become a pearl. You look at the world and you try to see as many levels of meaning there as you can. You ask, What else can it be? You develop what Flannery O'Connor called anagogical vision, a religious term meaning you're able to see different levels of reality in a single image or situation. The way that Mrs. Turpin in "Revelation" sees that the hogs she's hosing down are her salvation. You give your imagination opportunities. You present it with as many images, concepts, ideas, words, people, and paradoxes as you can—some will fire the brain. You know that the best way to have a good idea is to have lots of ideas. You trust both your imagination (that which connects) and your story to lead you.

You can't write fiction while being logical. Stories are not imagined with logic. Logic doesn't leap, it plods. It's necessary later, but not at the start.

Logic understands that which is:

 Consistent

Non-contradictory

 Certain

Ordered

But life is:

 Ambiguous

Contradictory

 Inconsistent

Chaotic

Thinking is about making connections, seeing the random heap of sweepings that Heraclitus saw and imposing a beautiful order on them—the way the first stargazers looked up and saw the bear, the lion, and the hunter in that impossibly hectic sky.

You can't wait for inspiration. You have to go after it with a club.

–Jack London

More on "Inspiration"

The muse, if she exists, comes only to the writing desk. She's not hanging out at the pub or in the TV room or at the fabulous party. In other words, you don't wait, you write. There are many people who want to have written. Writers want to write. We don't have trouble sitting down at the desk. We have trouble getting up from the desk. We do so only when sometimes we have to go find new material or talk to some like-minded folks about writing and literature. On the other hand, inspiration understood as "stimulation of the mind or emotion to a high level of feeling or activity" is crucial to a writer. In that sense, trouble is inspiration.

A student of mine once dropped by the house and told me he was getting a divorce. His marriage of two years was clearly not working out. I told him I was sorry to hear that, and then I said, "Take notes; you'll be writing about this for the rest of your life." In fact, I probably gave the advice before I offered my condolences and a stiff drink.

Trouble may be inspiring, but it's difficult to write well when you're troubled. That's another romantic notion: the myth of the anguished and starving writer. If you have no money, you will not be thinking about your plot because you'll be thinking about where your next meal is coming from—and you'll be busy doing something about securing it. If your marriage is in crisis or your child is suffering a terminal illness, the serenity and the time needed to write will not be available to you. You may write about the death of a loved one, but perhaps not while you're grieving. Wordsworth wrote: "Poetry is the spontaneous overflow of powerful feelings: it takes its origin from emotion recollected in tranquility." You need some distance from the trouble in order to understand it clearly.

Don't go looking for trouble! But take everything that is toxic and menacing and give it all to your characters, and do what you can to keep what is malignant out of your own life. Trouble will come; you don't have to court it.

Fortunately, personal trouble is not a prerequisite for writing. But your story is always about trouble, and trouble is all around us. Any unhappy family will do. Open the newspaper, turn on the news. Someone's in trouble. Every nine seconds a woman in this country reports being abused. Every single minute a woman dies from complications of pregnancy or childbirth. There are fifteen thousand or so murders in the U.S. every year.

A man wearing a portable oxygen tank, with tubes in his nose, robs a bank. The superintendent of schools is busted for child pornography. And so on. How and why did that happen? What drove an eighty-one-year-old woman to hold up a 7-Eleven? Just this morning, two people (my sister, who knows my interests, and Mollie, a writer friend who lives in Dripping Springs, Texas, and recognizes a good story) sent me a link to the same article, one that I had not seen:

A ninety-one-year-old widow in rural Pennsylvania lived with the corpses of her husband of sixty years and her twin sister. She had had the bodies exhumed just days after each burial. For over ten years, her deceased husband lay or sat in a dark suit, white shirt, and blue knitted tie on a couch in a detached garage. Her sister reposed on a couch in a spare room, dressed in her best housedress. The widow sprayed the room with her sister's favorite perfume. "I put glasses on her. When I put the glasses on, it made all the difference in the world. I would fix her up. I'd fix her face up all the time." When asked why she did it, the widow said that death was very hard for her. And then someone tipped off the police, who removed the bodies. And now she's alone again. This is certainly a story worth exploring. Who dug up those bodies and kept her secret? What did she talk about with her twin? How did she keep the world away from her door? How will she go on?

Art is also inspiration. When I read a heartbreaking story or listen to sublime music or watch a spellbinding movie, I want to run to the desk and try to shape a story that will enchant and transport my reader in the way I was just transported. If culture is everything we don't have to do, then art is doing what we don't have to do with absolute honesty. Estimable art is unprecedented and singular. It deepens the mystery, amplifies the world, and provokes both a state of wonder and a sense of kinship. It vitalizes and stimulates and is a resounding affirmation of life. It is, we might say, miraculous and transformative. So get in the habit of exposing yourself to great art. Who has not gazed on Ansel Adams' *Moonrise over Hernandez, New Mexico*, for example, and wondered, *Who lives in that adobe house to the left, the large one looking out over the sagebrush and the cemetery? Every day she looks out on the graves of her husband and her children. She says her prayers and rouses the grandchildren for their breakfast before school.* And now your story has begun. And now you see the children, hiding under bedcovers, trying to get back to their dreams and keep the tedious world away for a little longer.

Creating art is, itself, also inspirational. You see a woman enter your fictional kitchen; you look closely; you see that she has something in her hand; you want to know what it is; you have to know, but she won't show it to you; it's her secret, she says. Okay, then, you'll write the scene in which her delicious secret is revealed. And that scene will inspire the next scene, and so on. The more you write, the more you want to write, the more you miss it when your so-called real life summons you away from the desk. Soon you are falling asleep thinking of your darlings and waking up, grabbing your coffee, and rushing to the writing desk to see what they're up to.

If they give you ruled paper, write the other way.

–Ray Bradbury

Exercise 1:

Here and Now

Write about where you are physically right now. In the writing room or the kitchen, in a theater, on the subway. Pay attention to what's around you. Gaze. Write in first person, present tense. The smell and the sounds. Keep jotting down sense experience. What about the textures of things? What does the seat feel like? What do you see now that you didn't see before? How could you have missed it? What else have you been missing all your life?

Exercise 2:

There and Then

Think about the place where you grew up, and, of course, the time you grew up there. How was that place different from any other place, than the place you live now? And even if you haven't moved geographically, the place has changed, hasn't it? What were the local rituals that made it unique? Think about language, vocabulary, dialect, accent. Think about foods; think about the work people did. Remember the annual events that everyone looked forward to. The landscape, the architecture, the town or the neighborhood legends and characters. This could be the setting for stories, remember. Walk around the town or the neighborhood and put your five senses to work. Stop and talk to the people you find there—the people from your own past. Think about the seasons, the light, the ground, the schools, the churches, the secret places you escaped to.

Exercise 3:

The Shoe That Drops

You are aware that something is missing in your life. And it's not money. It's something more important than that. What is it? Or who is it? Don't resist it now. It can't hurt you. No one else needs to know. Something (someone) you've never had or something (someone) you've had and you've lost. It is a hollowness that eats at your heart. It's what you think about when you're sitting alone in a quiet room, and it's three a.m., and you can't sleep. It's the shoe that drops and snaps you out of your dreams. It's what you remember just when you think everything in your life is going so well. Or perhaps, when you consider dying, you think: *This is what I need before it's too late.* Write about this void, give this emptiness a shape.

Chapter Two

The Fiction Writing

Collaborate with the Reader

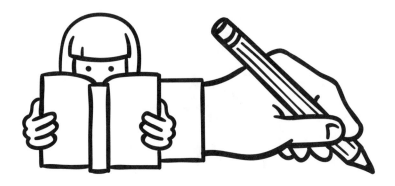

A story is a *collaborative* endeavor. You provide the clues, a river, say, and stand a character neck-deep in that river, and your reader sees the arrow of ripples around the character's body, sees the gunmetal gray of the water. Umberto Eco put it this way: "Every text is a lazy machine asking the reader to do some of its work." The point is this: that the making of a story is partly the achievement of the reader. It's our creative collaboration as readers that accounts for the fact that no other narrative art can move us like fiction, can take us out of our world and drop us into a world more brilliant and intense. We lose our sense of time, and we resent the return to our mundane lives.

So you, the writer, want your reader to be not passively observing but actively participating in the creation. You want her leaning in, not sitting back. You can do this in many ways, but here are five basic strategies.

**Make the Reader
See Your Characters**

 **Don't Tell the Reader
Everything**

 **Surprise
the Reader**

 **Create
Suspense**

 **Write Powerful
Emotional Moments**

My task is by the power of the word to make you hear, to make you feel– it's before all, to make you see.

–Joseph Conrad

Make the Reader See Your Characters

If you want your reader to see your character, and, trust me, you do, don't do what might be the first thing that pops to mind and describe the character. Description is static and denies the reader the chance to get in on the creation of the story. Better: put your character in motion. When the character moves, the reader's imagination is triggered. You write, "Diane lifted the coffee cup to her lips with both hands and gazed across the table at this man who had so recently and so suddenly walked into her life," and the reader sees the cup, the steam rising off the coffee, sees Diane's brown eyes, thin nose, sees her elbows resting on the table and the smile dawning on her lips, and so on.

Imagination is, perhaps, our most fundamental mode of thought. We see or taste or touch or hear or smell what is not present to our senses. Consider Albert Einstein's statement: "I very rarely think in words at all." And, "The words or language, as they are written or spoken, do not seem to play any role in my mechanism of thought." Words are abstract; images are concrete. Here's Temple Grandin: "I think in pictures. Words are like a second language to me. I translate both spoken and written words into full-color movies, complete with sound, which run like a VCR tape in my head. When somebody speaks to me, his words are instantly translated into pictures."

This notion of the movie playing in Temple Grandin's head reminds me of John Gardner's explanation of how fiction does its work—by creating a vivid and continuous dream in the reader's mind. The writer makes the dream vivid by presenting the reader with as many concrete images as possible, makes the dream continuous by avoiding anything that might distract the reader from the dream, a slip of technique, for instance, or an unwarranted authorial intrusion.

Let's take a moment to consider this matter of visual thinking. Vision is the most sophisticated and highly developed of our five-plus senses, and our brains have become powerful tools for processing and storing our visual images. Thirty percent of the neurons in the cerebral cortex are devoted to vision (as opposed to only two percent for hearing). This visual imagery is the real language of the brain, not the abstract constructions we call words. In his groundbreaking book *Visual Thinking*, Rudolph Arnheim wrote: "Thinking calls for images, and images contain thought."

Dreams are a daily way that we think visually. Words in dreams are relatively unimportant and in some cases not there at all. You might practice visual thinking by writing out your dreams in the morning. Describe the images and consider their significance. What were those seven blue cats doing in the wheelbarrow? Memories are another daily, almost constant way we think visually. Recall where you were when you learned of the World Trade Center disaster, and you see where you were and see what you did when you understood the horror.

Another way to practice visual thinking is by drawing or sketching the places you find yourself spending time at. This is to help you remember the places, to reinforce the images you're looking at, not to necessarily make exquisite works of art, though you might do that as well. This hotel room you're sitting in could be the hotel room your character, a woman running for her life, is sitting and fretting in. Drawing the room, no matter how crudely, will help you remember all of the details of the room, even those that did not make it into the sketch. And this is yet another reason to carry that notebook with you.

Close your eyes and see the image provoked by a word like *justice*. You might see a judge in a black robe, gavel in hand, or balanced scales. The point is you can't see the concept, justice, and you can't hear, taste, touch, or smell it. The fiction writer wants to portray a concept, an emotion, an idea, but she has to do so dramatically, by showing, by somehow embodying the idea. You might want to try this out right now before going on to the next paragraph. Try the idea-to-image exercise with these words: *love, death, joy, spirit*. And maybe write about the significance of the image that popped into your head. Why the valentine heart for love and not your mother?

Here's a way to think of your job as a writer. Your job is to take the images you see so clearly in reality or in your imagination and find the words to present the images so that the reader can see them just as sharply.

Don't Tell the Reader Everything

What you leave out of your story is at least as important as what you leave in. British novelist Henry Green said, "The more you leave out, the more you highlight what you leave in." Michelangelo put it this way: "The more the marble wastes, the more the statue grows." And here's Ernest Hemingway espousing his Theory of Omission in *A Moveable Feast*: "I omitted the end [of the story "Out of Season"] which was that the old man hanged himself. This was omitted on my new theory that you could omit anything if you knew that you omitted and the omitted part would strengthen the story." The key is, I think, that you have to know already; you have to have written about what it is you're going to toss out. You have to write a lot to write a little.

William Trevor, who began his artistic life as a sculptor, speaks to this point. "If there's not enough to throw away, you've got to make some more . . . throwing away is . . . the most vital part, and the most exciting part of writing is what you decide should not be there, and you've got left what you want . . . " You need to write much more than the reader will have to read. This is a brave new world you are creating with each story, and you're not God, so it's going to take you a lot longer than seven days to get it done. You must throw away a huge amount of material. Think of this material as the matrix (from the Latin for *womb*) in which your story is nourished and nurtured. Or think of what you'll leave out as the ninety percent of the iceberg below the surface. We may not see it, but it floats the ten percent we do see.

But how do you decide what to throw out? Before we attempt an answer, let's consider how a writer whose job it is to be mindful of her fictive world, to pay attention, and to notice everything, might examine and explore a character's seemingly obvious and perhaps even trivial behavior by slowing that behavior down.

Your central character, Nevin, we'll call him, stands on a busy city sidewalk, takes out his cell phone, and calls his wife. He wants to tell her he'll be later than usual getting home from work. The call itself is integral to the plot and cannot be cut, but you realize the paragraph you wrote is flat and isn't breathing on the page, and you didn't even learn anything new about Nevin—so neither will the reader. The incident of the sidewalk phone call begs for your attention. You understand that you now have the opportunity, in your notebook, to learn more about Nevin and about this important moment by looking closely and by writing down what you observe and what you make of these observations. In so doing you're teaching yourself to see. You ask yourself, *What did I miss the first time?* This looking back, this process of serial regression, is essential to the storytelling process. Let's do some revision, some re-seeing, right now.

Nevin keeps his iPhone in the left front pocket of his khaki chinos. Is he left-handed? It's too bright to see the screen in the glaring sunlight, so Nevin ducks into the entryway of the building behind him. Before he makes his call, you take a look at his screensaver—Edward Hopper's *Nighthawks*. You're pleased at your discovery. Nevin is an art lover who shares your own love of Hopper. Might as well check his apps. Lots of photography, productivity, and sports. And he's got the app you've always wanted but didn't know existed, iWhimper, the one where the phone wails like an infant if you get more than four feet away from it. Maybe you'll scroll through Nevin's photos later. And you'll empty that messenger bag he has slung over his shoulder.

By the way, you're writing all this down as quickly as you can without any particular regard for grammar, punctuation, or mechanics. One image will lead you to another. Trust the process. Nevin presses his wife's cell phone number. He waits. He notices two bald men in blue shorts and white T-shirts, with hankies on their heads, walk by. They're twins, you decide. Bachelors. They share an apartment in Old Town. You wonder if you can find a place for these guys in the novel. Nevin wishes he weren't holding the phone to his ear, so he could snap a photo of these two. He listens for the beep and he leaves his message. He sees Frida waving to him from across Main Street. Who's Frida? Is she Nevin's secret? You'll find out. You'll take what you just learned about Nevin and apply it to your plot. The rest you may disregard for the time being.

Now that you've seen one way that an abundance of raw material can be generated, and you also realize you can never know enough about each of your characters, and you're going to have to walk around this place you've created, this city, town, or trailer park, so you can know it as well as the native you are, and all this material accumulates, and all of it is informing the story, but not all of it belongs on the page, the question becomes: what do I discard? Here are a few things to leave out.

Leave out anything that happened before the trouble begins. Start as close to the end of the story as you can, when everything but the action is over.

Leave out anything that happens after the central character's problem has been resolved. No stories should end with "and they all lived happily ever after." We don't care and we don't believe it.

Leave out any line that you love, but that is not crucial to the story. Heed Arthur Quiller-Couch's advice: "Murder your darlings." Don't show off. If the line is only there because it's clever, get rid of it.

Leave out any images, any details, that are not both vivid and significant.

Leave out any scenes, conversations, descriptions, images that are not doing two of these three things:

1. Advancing the plot

2. Revealing character

3. Expressing theme

Leave out anything the reader can assume.

Here's an example of leaving out what the reader can assume, which gives me a chance to talk about the Synaptic Theory of Composition and begin a transition to the third way to encourage collaboration: surprise the reader.

Synapse is from the Greek *synapsis*, point of contact. Specifically, a synapse in the brain is a small gap or junction separating two neurons. (There are 100 billion neurons in the human brain, capable of making 100 trillion connections.) In order for a message to travel from one neuron to another there needs to be a gap between them. Think of a spark plug: no gap, no fire, no ignition, no go. You don't want the snug joinery of logic here. You want the movement loose, disjointed; you want the imaginative leap across the microchasm. You want the surprise between every word, sentence, paragraph, and chapter. Give the reader the unexpected, and she will pay attention.

Perhaps I learned the Synaptic Theory from watching movies, because the theory is not unlike Sergei Eisenstein's theory of montage, meaning the unity of shots of seemingly unrelated objects in the same film sequence so that they take on a new relationship to each other in the viewer's mind. Eisenstein came up with the idea and wrote about it in his essay "The Montage of Attractions."

He was influenced by his study of the Japanese written language, where two seemingly unrelated symbols, say *grain* and *fire*, are used together to form the word *autumn*. That's a way of metaphorical thinking that we as writers want to cultivate and develop. The whole is greater than the sum of its parts. It is the juxtaposition that makes the meaning.

grain + fire = autumn

So it's the contrast between the images that moves the story forward, that allows for the reader to fill in, to connect, what at first might seem arbitrary. Here's a simple example from a story of mine. In the story "The Freezer Jesus," the first-person narrator Arlis Elrod says:

> *And then comes that Friday and I'm walking Elvie up the path from the bean field at dusk and I notice the porch light on and I tell Elvie we must have had a visitor stop by. As we get closer I notice a blemish on the freezer door that wasn't there before. Then suddenly the blemish erupts like a volcano and commences to changing shape, and what were clouds at first become a beard and hair, and I recognize immediately and for certain that image is the very face of Jesus right down to the mole near his left eye.*
>
> *What is it, Arlis? Elvie says to me. Why you shaking? Of course Elvie can't see what I see because she's blind as a snout beetle. So I tell her about this Jesus and somehow she knows it's true and falls to her knees and sobs.*

Then I write about Arlis's thoughts and how this is the oddest thing that's ever happened in Holly Ridge, Louisiana. And Elvie tells him to call the newspaper. And in the next scene a reporter comes out and checks it all out and writes his piece. Now the reader knows that Arlis did what he was told to do, even though she didn't see it, and she didn't need his thoughts to understand. She immediately imagined a phone call to the city desk at the *News-Star-World*. Don't tell the reader what she doesn't need to know. Don't tell her what she can assume.

A slight digression on this matter of thinking illogically, of letting the arbitrary guide you. The concept was, as far as I know, first expressed by the French writer Paul Souriau, who said, "Pour inventer, il faut penser à côté." To invent you should think sideways.

Divergent, oblique, sidewise, or lateral thinking goes away from choosing the next logical step; it invites completely irrelevant ideas to intrude on the continuity of patterned thinking. From these intrusions come disconnected, off-the-wall ideas that may seem unrelated to the problem until suddenly they generate creative and exceptional solutions.

We normally think in patterns that are predictable and repetitive, and the idea of divergent thinking and the idea of arbitrary structures is to break down those patterns. Arthur Koestler defined lateral thinking as a "shift of attention to some feature of the situation, or an aspect of the problem, which was previously ignored, or only present on the fringes of awareness."

So if you're stuck, and every idea you come up with seems like a cliché, or it's too predictable, open a dictionary to any page. The first noun defined on the page or in the second column or wherever you decide is your unblocking word. Play with all its meanings for a few minutes and see what wild, uncalculated connections they might have for your original problem.

Surprise the Reader

The unexpected is the fiction writer's best weapon of suspense. This is the reader's cerebral involvement with the story. The reader says, *I know what's going to happen next*, and then waits to see, and if he ever does guess right, then the story's over for him. Keep the reader guessing and engaged.

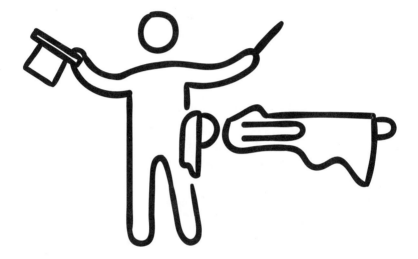

Because we fiction writers are writing about what we don't understand, our writing is exploration and discovery, and what we discover, naturally, surprises us. The surprise is what brings us to the desk every day. And our surprises in creation become surprises in our stories, surprises that will both create tension and engage the reader's attention. A surprise might be a robust verb, an unpredictable behavior by a character, an abrupt shift in time or place, a plot point that spins the action of the story off in a new direction, or an unexpected turn of events. And maybe there should be at least one surprise on every page. The word *surprise* began its life with a military meaning, "to overtake, seize, or invade," but came to mean a more familiar "overpowering of the emotions." And surprise as we know it is nearly always accompanied by delight.

There will come a moment in the writing of your story when the central character will surprise you. He'll do something you did not expect him to do or will say something you didn't expect him to say. And when that happens, while you may be perplexed, you will also perk up, pay attention, and, perhaps, smile. This is the moment when you know that you have a story, when you know you have created a character and not a caricature, a person and not a puppet. This is when the real writing begins. Surprise commands attention and provokes a sense of wonder. *How did that just happen?* you ask yourself. I don't know, but I'm glad it did. Now you can follow the character around and write down what he does and says as you keep putting obstacles in his way.

Surprise means to affect strongly and suddenly; to seize; to arouse astonishment. One of your jobs is to present your reader with the unexpected so that she will perk up and pay attention. We are not reading a story to be told what we already know, what we expect. The surprises can be lexical, the use of what Ford Madox Ford called "the fresh, usual words." You know the word *placid*, but you've never seen it used to describe coddled eggs before. The surprise can be metaphorical, where the unobvious attributes of one object (the vehicle) are used to describe the other (the tenor). "All the world's a stage," Shakespeare wrote. The more apt and surprising your comparison, the better your metaphor. The surprises in the story can also be psychological or emotional. Your character does not respond to stress in the way you thought she might. The surprise might be narrative: a shift in the action that the reader was not expecting. But your ending should not be a complete surprise in this sense. What you want is that your resolution be unpredictable, of course, but also inevitable. The reader could not have seen it coming, but now cannot imagine it being otherwise.

Create Suspense

Suspense is defined as mental uncertainty, anxiety, and apprehension. Alfred Hitchcock, in an interview with François Truffaut, explained the difference between surprise and suspense:

> There is a distinct difference between "suspense" and "surprise," and yet many pictures continually confuse the two. I'll explain what I mean. We are now having a very innocent little chat. Let's suppose that there is a bomb underneath this table between us. Nothing happens, and then all of a sudden, "Boom!" There is an explosion. The public is surprised, but prior to this surprise, it has seen an absolutely ordinary scene, of no special consequence. Now, let us take a suspense situation. The bomb is underneath the table and the public knows it, probably because they have seen the anarchist place it there. The public is aware the bomb is going to explode at one o'clock and there is a clock in the decor. The public can see that it is a quarter to one. In these conditions, the same innocuous conversation becomes fascinating because the public is participating in the scene. The audience is longing to warn the characters on the screen: "You shouldn't be talking about such trivial matters. There is a bomb beneath you and it is about to explode!" In the first case we have given the public fifteen seconds of surprise at the moment of the explosion. In the second we have provided them with fifteen minutes of suspense. The conclusion is that whenever possible the public must be informed. Except when the surprise is a twist, that is, when the unexpected ending is, in itself, the highlight of the story.

About plot and suspense, E. M. Forster, in *Aspects of the Novel*, wrote, "Yes—oh dear yes—the novel tells a story." And went on wonderfully to explain the need for plot:

The Fiction Writing

Neanderthal man listened to stories . . . The primitive audience was an audience of shock-heads, gaping around the campfire, fatigued with contending against the mammoth or the woolly rhinoceros, and only kept awake by suspense. What would happen next? The novelist droned on, and as soon as the audience guessed what happened next, they either fell asleep or killed him. We can estimate the dangers incurred when we think of the career of Scheherazade in somewhat later time. Scheherazade avoided her fate because she knew how to wield the weapon of suspense—the only literary tool that has any effect upon tyrants and savages.

Perhaps Forster's key word here is *suspense*, the pleasurable excitement and anticipation regarding an outcome. That's what plot affords the reader. We don't know where we're going, and we're desperate to find out. Plot suggests that this tale we're reading is a journey we're on, that each narrative step we take leads to the next step, and that all of our trudging will carry us to the story's ultimate destination, which, for now, remains a mystery. If we understand that we're going somewhere, and we sense that that somewhere promises to be intriguing, then we'll keep on going. We don't need or want to know the specific destination; we just need the assurance that there is one. If we guess the destination, in fact, as Forster points out, we'll be angry or bored. A plot makes the reader want to know what happens next. And that's a good thing. And we'll talk more about plot later.

The novelist Lee Child, in a *New York Times* essay, offered this advice for creating suspense: Ask a question at the beginning of the story or novel, and then delay the answer. Humans, and readers are humans, "are programmed to wait for answers to questions they witness being asked." The basic narrative fuel, he writes, is the slow unveiling of the final answer.

Ask "Who did it?" on page one and reveal the answer in the last chapter.

Write Powerful Emotional Moments

We may read nonfiction for information, but we read fiction for understanding. And what we want to understand is what it's like to be a human being and how that feels. We read stories to be moved, to be roused, to be touched, and to be carried away. We want to feel something because we spend much of our time absorbed with our work and our social obligations and the rest of our time distracted by all of the anesthetizing electronic devices we've happily cluttered our lives with. We're numbed by our amusements and our responsibilities, and we don't want to be. We turn to stories. We read to share the emotions of the characters so that we know we are alive and we are not alone, and in that realization we may be renewed and restored.

The actress Rosalind Russell said, "Do you know what makes movies work? Moments. Give the audience half a dozen moments they can remember, and they'll leave the theater happy." Think *novels* and *reader*. In order to write these moments, you first have to make the reader care about your characters. To do that you have to let the reader get to know the character. The better the reader knows the character, the more he'll understand, admire, and root for the character. Characters are the emotional center of stories. It is the characters who teach us what love is, what death is. It is through character that we come to know ourselves and to understand what we're doing, or what we think we're doing. These powerful emotional moments will always come in scene. And in those scenes you will scrupulously avoid sentimentality and attend to subtext. You'll utilize tone and pace, setting and ambience, to make your meaning. We'll talk more about scenes and about just what makes them work when we discuss plot.

Writer's Block

There are letter blocks for learning the alphabet. There are building blocks and city blocks, stumbling blocks, and butcher blocks. There are blocks and tackles both in football and in hoisting, You can block a punch or block a hat. There are starting blocks and block letters. But there is no writer's block. What has been called writer's block is simply an excuse not to write. If you didn't write today, it's because you chose not to, not because you are blocked, not that you have a strange neurological condition that only affects writers and is untreatable, but temporary.

Yes, we all feel anxiety and emotional distress, and we're unhappy some of the time, angry and irritated at other times. Some days we're apathetic and disengaged. Other days we're disappointed with our creative abilities. We wonder if we've lost our mojo, finally. Our motivation flags. We're mired in a slough of doubt. We don't feel the joy we once felt when writing. Our only recourse, we think, is we'll have to wait this out. And maybe a drink will help us pass the downtime. Or a trip to Paris. Didn't Kafka say that a non-writing writer was a monster courting insanity? And then we remember we're adults, and nothing can stop us from writing if we don't want it to. So what do we do if we can't seem to get started?

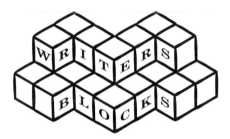

First, what not to do. We do not name this temporary condition "writer's block," thereby rendering it legitimate and powerful. We know that this lull is part of the writing process. We'll call it gestation if we need a name. We remind ourselves that the finest work comes from the hardest struggle. We let that sustain us. And then we write about what's stopping us from writing. Write it in that notebook we carry with us. Problem solved. Put down a word. Any word. Put down another. And soon the pump is primed and we're back at the scene in the story that first discouraged us.

The TV show *The Golden Girls* famously addressed this matter of writer's block:

Blanche:
Well, now I know why Hemingway killed himself. Oh, girls, I have writer's block. This is the worst feeling in the world.

Sophia:
Try ten days without a bowel movement sometime.

Blanche:
You just sit there hour after hour after hour.

Sophia:
Tell me about it.

Blanche:
I just don't know what to do. I don't think there's any worse feeling in the world than facing that blank piece of paper.

Dorothy:
Tell me, how much have you written so far?

Blanche:
Well, that's just it. Nothing. That's how I know I have writer's block.

Dorothy:
Blanche, you have to have written to have writer's block. Otherwise, all of us have it.

KEEP CALM AND WRITE ON

The Ten Commandments
of Writing Fiction:

1. Sit your ass in the chair!

2. Thou shalt not bore the reader.

3. Remember to keep holy your writing time.

4. Honor the lives of your characters.

5. Thou shalt not be obscure.

6. Thou shalt show and not tell.

7. Thou shalt steal!

8. Thou shalt rewrite and rewrite again. And again.

9. Thou shalt confront the human condition.

10. Be sure that every death in a story means something!

The Three Cardinal Sins*
of the Fiction Writer:

Sentimentality

Frigidity

Mannerism

* According to John Gardner

Sentimentality

The dictionary tells us that sentimentality is an "an excess of sentiment; mawkishly emotional; indulging in feeling to an inordinate extent." Sentiment is honest emotion or feeling and is essential to fiction. (We want our readers to feel as well as to think—but we don't want to tell them how to feel or what to think.) Sentimentality is a false, cloying, and superficial emotion. It relies on the reader's emotional experience rather than on the experience the writer creates in the narrative.

Sentimentality, Gardner writes in *The Art of Fiction*, is "emotion or feeling that rings false" because it is achieved "by some form of cheating or exaggeration." The sentimental writer then tries to get some effect without due cause. The writer wants us to cry, for example, about a character we don't know well enough to care about, or he appeals to stock responses or tries to make us cry with novelettish melodrama. He writes, "Large, sorrowful tears poured down her pallid cheeks" instead of, "She cried." His diction is fustian, blustery, bombastic, and intimidating. Better to heed Chekhov's advice here. "When you describe the miserable and unfortunate, and want to make the reader feel pity, try to be somewhat colder—that seems to give a kind of background to another's grief, against which it stands out more clearly. Whereas in your story the characters cry and you sigh. Yes, be more cold . . . The more objective you are, the stronger will be the impression you make."

Frigidity

Gardner writes, "The fault Longinus identified as 'frigidity' occurs in fiction whenever the author reveals by some slip or self-regarding intrusion that he is less concerned about his characters than he ought to be—less concerned, that is, than any decent human being observing the situation would naturally be." Frigidity may be said to be a lack of imagination, emotional timidity, a deficiency of nerve or spirit. Frigid prose might be described as lacking warmth of feeling, of being stiff, formal, tawdry, and affected. The writer who will not take the time to revise, to find the precise verb as opposed to the serviceable verb, is frigid. When a responsible writer settles for writing a potboiling piece of novelese, he is frigid. Frigidity characterizes the writer who presents serious material and then fails to carry through with it, to give it the attention it demands and deserves. If you are going to tell the story of a difficult divorce, then you are going to have to deal with all of the confusing and painful emotions that your characters will experience. You have a contract with the reader, and you ought not to violate it.

Mannerism

Mannerism is excessive or affected addiction to a distinctive manner of treatment, characterized by stylistic exaggeration. The mannered writer pays more attention to his own presence in the story than to that of the characters or the plot. His self-congratulatory stylistics distract and detract from the story. This is the writer who says watch what I can do. He is addicted to an excessive or self-conscious use of a distinctive and usually florid prose style. He's a show-off, impressed with his own cleverness. Here's a writer with an unquenchable thirst for originality, who has no idea what originality is. Being different is not being original. Originality is not affectation.

Writers who commit these cardinal sins share certain self-regarding elements. They have not learned a basic tenet of fiction writing: the reader doesn't care, and shouldn't care, about the author. The reader cares about the characters in the story. Better to heed Flaubert's advice that the writer in her work should be like God in his creation, invisible and all-powerful, everywhere felt, but nowhere seen.

The First Draft

Getting black on white

A typical page of one of my own first drafts:

Stories and novels don't get written. They get rewritten. Most matters of consequence in fiction are addressed in revisions. And the most essential fact about revision is that you have to have something to revise.

One route's a task.
The other's a pleasure.

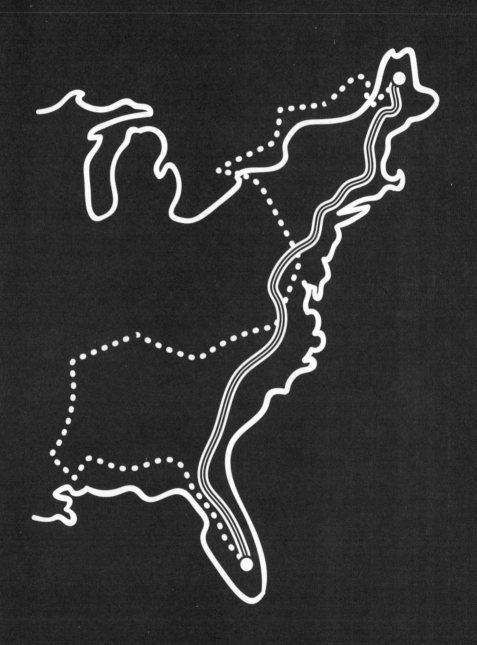

Life is a journey!
So is a first draft!

You begin writing the story not knowing where you will end up. You may have a destination in mind, and you may set off in that direction. You can make a beeline if you're in a hurry or you can wander. Which is more interesting? Which will lead to discovery and surprise? Which will take longer? You'll learn more about your world taking the circuitous route. And, in either case, what you encounter along the way will alter your course. To drive from New York to Miami, you can take I-95 (and wave to Pedro at South of the Border), or you can drive via Montreal, Memphis, and New Orleans . . . You wind up in the same place—but, ah! the journey . . .

As a writer you are a traveler in a newfound land. You're what the French call a flâneur or flâneuse, a wanderer, an idler, a stroller who aimlessly loses herself in a crowd, taking in all the rich detail of your story, going wherever curiosity leads you, collecting impressions along the way. A first draft is about research and exploration. It is not a time to hurry, but to linger. Get off the highways and onto the byways. Apply the brakes, pull off the road. Meet the locals. Sample the regional cuisines. Note the architecture and the landscape. All of these discoveries will find their way into your story. The journey is the destination.

And speaking of travel:

When we travel, visit new places, we tend to be alert, to notice things that we might not ordinarily pay attention to. We notice the unusual flora and fauna, the peculiar architectural details, the illuminating local customs, the strange food, the exotic aromas. Travel trains us to notice. We are open to new experiences; we welcome new interaction with people. We are assertively curious. Everything we see attracts our attention. We are, in fact, a lot like fiction writers when we are travelers. And that's a state we want to try to foster in our daily lives. To be travelers when we're at home.

Why do we travel?

As Mark Twain said, "Travel is fatal to prejudice, bigotry, and narrow-mindedness, and many of our people need it sorely on these accounts. Broad, wholesome, charitable views of men and things cannot be acquired by vegetating in one little corner of the earth all one's lifetime." He also said, "The world is a book and those who do not travel read only one page."

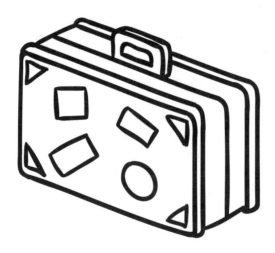

Don't think you know what the story is before you write it. You're not a puppetmaster. You're a scribe writing down what your characters do, say, and think.

I write any sort of rubbish which will cover the main outlines of the story, then I can begin to see it.

–Frank O'Connor

A first draft should be easy:

You have nothing to prove.

You have nothing to defend.

You're bringing something new into the world that did not exist.

No one has to see it.

You write it for yourself.

But writing a first draft is not easy! It takes:

Faith

Grit

Boldness

Resilience

Poise

Good fortune

The ability to accept failure

The first draft separates the wannabes from the writers. Writers are those who are not stopped, or even fazed, by failure. Why? Because that is where the trouble starts.

Consider the sea squirt

You can be adventurous in your life and in your writing; you can explore the worlds around you, or you can settle for being a marine saclike, hermaphroditic filter-feeder, the sea squirt, and attach yourself to a rock where you'll spend the rest of your life. Finish your journey before it begins. First thing you do is eat your brain because you don't need it anymore. True fact, as they say. Eat your backbone, too. Eat your eye. Who needs it now?

What the curious behavior of the sea squirt suggests is that our brains may have evolved to choreograph our movement and exploration. And, perhaps, the more we move, the more complex and robust our brains become. We have evolved to do more than eat and reproduce. We want to understand the mysteries around us and to make sense of the apparent chaos. We're on a journey from uncertainty toward meaning, and we can't do that while stuck to a rock.

The first draft
of a book is the
most uncertain—
where you need
guts, the ability
to accept the
imperfect until it
is better.

–Bernard Malamud

Life may be spontaneous, but art is not!

Getting started

The first draft is where the beginning writer most often finds himself stuck, discouraged, and doomed. He gives himself an F grade for his faltering efforts and clumsy execution and takes the grade seriously. What had seemed like a noble adventure now seems like a fool's errand. This novice I'm thinking of is the person—you've met him at parties—who claims to have dozens of scintillating and compelling ideas for stories. He can describe his story to you—and he will as soon as he discovers you're a writer—in elaborate detail. It's most often about his own experiences. He may be able to articulate theme, explain how he'll go about revealing character, lay in symbols, build tension, unfurl the plot. But he never gets the story written, though he feels an urgency to do so. Often it is this very urgency that aborts the narrative. This novice writer wants to dodge the drafting process and write the story immediately. He doesn't know what every experienced fiction writer knows: that the story does not exist before the act of writing, that it emerges through the flow of images and the rhythm of words, and the rhyming of events. He fails to understand that while life might be spontaneous, art is not.

And so he makes mistakes. He sets unrealistic goals for what he may not acknowledge to be, but is, in fact, only the first draft. He undermines his effort by holding unrealistic expectations of his imaginative and organizing powers. And so he becomes discouraged when the people in his head are unrecognizable on the page, when the intense emotion he felt in real life is unrealized in what he writes. The beginning writer who has read a great deal is even more susceptible to this kind of dejection. She knows that the García Márquez story she just read did not flounder the way hers seems to. She loses confidence and hope, becomes intimidated by the magnitude of the problem that is the nascent story, is humbled by her vaulting ambition, appalled by her hubris. She acknowledges the irretrievable breakdown of the creative venture and divorces herself from the enterprise.

What a shame to relinquish a dream over a misunderstanding. You were not supposed to get it right in the first draft; you were supposed to get it written. When your first draft is finished, you have only begun. Don't lament your failure; celebrate your achievement. You've done what very few people can do—you've written a beginning, a middle, and an end to a story.

All first drafts are shit!*

So what's the lesson?

Do not write beyond what the first draft is meant to accomplish.

Don't expect a finished manuscript.

Don't let your critic sit down with your editor.

Don't worry too much about the flow of the plot.

This is a new world—get to know the people who live there.

Do explore the world of your story.

If you want to care about your characters, you have to know them.

* Ernest Hemingway

When you're stuck:

 Freewrite

 Brainstorm

 Clustering

 The Next Word

 Tell Me a Secret

 # Freewrite

This technique was first mentioned, as far as I know, in a book called *Becoming a Writer* by Dorothea Brande, published in 1934. Pick up a pen and write about whatever is there, or about a suggested topic, and don't stop for five minutes or ten minutes or whatever. Set a timer so you don't have to look up. The secret here is not to think. Write quickly. Keep the pen moving. Doodle if you have to. Write what you think of as nonsense if you have to.

If you are stuck, write, "I'm stuck. I'm supposed to be writing about 'smoke' but I can't . . . " Just don't stop. And don't censor yourself. Don't worry where it's going. Follow the accident. The only way to go wrong here is to think. You're trying to move past your conscious thoughts to your unconscious—and until now, unarticulated—thoughts. The first time you do this is the hardest because you're so used to thinking and being analytical and all that.

Brainstorm

This list-making technique has been around for a while. It's based on the notion expressed by Nobel laureate Linus Pauling, who said, "The best way to get a good idea is to get lots of ideas." The goal is to come up with as many ideas as possible as quickly as possible. Brainstorming has traditionally been a group activity where one person's response triggers a response in another, and the energy created by the group propels the creative process. But you can also do it alone. You're stuck on your story. Let's say your character has just told his wife that he is leaving her. He walks out of their house. What does he do now?

Brainstorm the possibilities. Here are the rules. No criticism is allowed. Do not censor yourself. Everything and anything goes. Welcome crazy-seeming ideas. There is no such thing as a bad idea. Defer judgment until later. You have to be freewheeling and move beyond the conventional thought. Next, go for quantity. More is more. When you've generated a substantial list, look at the items and combine them and improve on them. Which of the items intrigues you the most? Go with that one.

Clustering

Here's another technique or exercise to get started or to get unblocked or to collect information for your story. Northrop Frye said that any word can "become a storm center of meanings, sounds, associations, radiating out indefinitely like ripples in a pool." This technique of clustering, or mapping, as it's called in some texts, addresses the preceding sentiment. It's an idea taken from Gabriele Rico's *Writing the Natural Way*. At least that's where I first saw it. It's based on the knowledge we have of the two hemispheres of the brain. The technique is similar to mind mapping, a colorful, visual network of words and associations.

This technique is based on word association. You know, the shrink says *dog*, and you say *cat*. She says *mother*, and you say *father*. She says *love*, and you say *wreckage* or whatever. In this case you begin with a word that you write on a blank page and circle. And then you write the first word suggested by the circled word and connect it to the first with a line. Then associate that word with the next and so on. When you come to a natural conclusion to that string of associations, go back to the original word and begin again. Don't think. Let your right brain associate. Don't stop moving the pen. Don't censor. First thing that comes into your head. So here's a word to start with. Write it in the middle of a blank page in your notebook, circle it, and go!

Loneliness.

As you fill up the page with associative words, some will surprise you, and that's as it should be. Don't try to make sense of where this word train is taking you. Soon enough, you will suddenly sense that you have something to write about. That is the intuitive leap that the exercise prompts. The right brain has been making patterns, making sense of all this. It can't do anything else. Stop, look back at the cluster for a starter word or sentence. Now write your sketch or your scene or whatever was suggested by the words. You're tapping into your unconscious, into your non-verbal mind. We have responses and opinions about everything, but we may not be aware (be conscious) of them. Now do another cluster in your notebook. Remember: Associate. Don't think. Write the word in the middle of the page.

Cluster on *fear*.

The Next Word

You're going to open your dictionary and select the fifth word in the second column (or whatever formula you decide on today). And then you're going to write the word down on a blank page and freewrite (as above) on the word until the page is full or for one minute or what you will. The secret here, once again, is not to think. Write fast. Open the dictionary, point your finger. Go!

(I just tried this. Gave myself a minute. Got *invertebrate* for my word, didn't think but wrote: *The blubbery slug who slimes his way across our sidewalk each morning and scales the house behind the hibiscus. Slugs don't seem to have backbones. At least at La Cucina I've never sensed a snap when I eat the escargot. Last time there, Felipe and I talked about Roma and Milano, and he ordered more garlic bread.* I hadn't thought about Felipe and his wife Nina in a while. Who'd have thought a slug would evoke their presence? One could do worse than start the writing day with a given word.)

Tell Me a Secret

Have a character tell you something about herself that you did not know, like, "I left home at sixteen." Now take advantage of your natural curiosity. Ask the questions that are suggested by the statement. "Why?" "Where did you go?" In fact, the traditional reporter's questions are a good place to start.

Who? What? When? Where? Why? and How? But gradually get more and more specific. The more specific the question, the more information is revealed in the answer. "What did you do when you got off the bus in Worcester?" Ask the questions and then let the character answer them as specifically as she can. This is how all fiction gets made. A writer learns which questions to ask. So, let's do one in your notebook. "Today, I decided to change my life." Ask the questions. Answer them. Begin the narrative if you have the time.

Give yourself fifteen minutes or thirty minutes. Set a timer. You have to, of course, invent the character who spoke those words. Name her. This is another exercise that you can use anytime you're bogged down in the writing process, just like freewriting and brainstorming.

Here's the opening to my story "The Fontana Gene":

When Billy Wayne Fontana's second wife, Tami Lynne, left him for the first time, he walked into Booker T. Washington Elementary School, interrupted the fourth grade in the middle of a hygiene lesson, it being a Thursday morning and all, apologized to Miss Azzie Lee Oglesbee, the substitute teacher, fetched his older boy Duane, and vanished for a year and a half from Monroe.

The line was a gift that appeared because I pushed the narrator, in this case, to tell me something about Billy Wayne that I didn't already know. Suddenly I had a father, a ten-year-old boy, at least one other male child, two wives, a town, submerged trouble, an eventual reconciliation, a second split, a kidnapping, a disappearance. I began to ask questions. What was it made Billy Wayne do something so desperate? Why would he take just the one boy? Why would Tami Lynne take him back? What would he do to make her leave again? What did he do and where did he go for a year and a half? Why did he come back? And what about that voice? Who is it telling this story? Not the narrator I thought I knew. I answered the questions for days, writing away in my notebook. I fiddled with structure and shape. Three months later I had an unwieldy first draft, but one that interested me immensely. Six months later I finished the story. Four years later I finished the novel that grew from the story. You might have a character, a young woman whose husband may leave her, tell you that when she was seven she wandered away from her family at the beach and wasn't found for hours. Ask the questions. Get specific. Let her answer them in detail.

The first draft is an exploration

So what if it takes you on tangents, leads you astray—that's its purpose! The purpose of the first draft is not to get it right but to get it written!

Trust the process

Writing is first of all a physical activity. An idea for a story is not a story. Thinking about writing is not writing. Telling your pals you're writing a story is not writing a story.

Some people want to have written; writers want to write. The process, the activity. Not the product. That's the job!

All of humanity's problems come from not being able to sit in a quiet room alone.

–Blaise Pascal

Writing is a way of thinking

[You don't think and then write.]

It both focuses and rattles the mind.

It concentrates your attention.

It's how you think best (if you're a writer).

And it's how you make sense of the world.

It is language distilled and refined.

It is speech that is concentrated, layered, coherent, textured, clear, stimulating, and resonant.

It is sitting alone in a quiet room.

It is choosing the work over distraction and diversion.

It is a plunge into reality, not an escape from it.

This is some of what we use to distract ourselves: radio, telephone, music, computer, texting, social media, TV, movies, shopping, driving, errands, parties, amusement parks—we clutter our lives to keep out of the quiet room and avoid the recognition of our mortality. But . . .

Death is the central fact of (and the end of) our existence—the sadness at our core. Everything we love will vanish. We can't hold on to anything. It is this tragedy that accounts as well for the beauty and nobility of our lives because in the face of this terrible knowledge, we go right on loving, trying to hold on to what we cherish, defying death with hubris and with faith.

So: introspection without distraction. You face the blank page with doubt and anxiety. Don't go to therapy—bring it all to the page. Insist on meaning, but not on answers, which aren't the point. The point is not to answer, but to question. Not to solve, but to seek; not to preach, but to explore; not to assure, but to agitate. Not to explain the mysteries of life, but to celebrate the mystery itself.

You create a reader and try to engage her imagination.

So: solitude and rumination. Your job is to be honest, clear, and fascinating. So you revise. Again and again. Bring doubt (a part of knowing) to the desk—it's what you don't know that counts because that ignorance engages your sense of wonder. So you drive through the uncertainty and arrive at what the poet Rumi called:

Astounded lucid confusion

Perseverance and patience, which you might think of as grace under pressure, are your most significant assets. You won't be stopped.

Man is in love and loves what vanishes, what more is there to say?

–William Butler Yeats

It's not that I'm so smart, it's just that I stay with problems longer.

–Albert Einstein

Plot

Here's a paraphrase of John Gardner's definition of a plot. You have a central character who wants something and goes after it despite opposition, and, as a result of a struggle, comes to a win or a loss. We're going to be talking extensively about plot very soon, but for now, just think about your writing a story as a plot. You want something—to understand the lives of your characters, which means resolving the trouble in your central character's life, which means completing the story—and you want it intensely. If you don't finish, your life will be significantly diminished, your self-esteem deflated, and your literary dreams deferred. And so you pursue your goal and battle every obstacle, not the least of which is yourself and your lack of confidence, your obstructionist tendencies, the world calling for your attention, the chaos of the characters' lives, those elusive words, and so on. You sit day after day. All important struggles are internal, you sense. You struggle and at last you finish your story. Or you don't. Plot's resolved, story's over.

Along the way you learn to cultivate ambiguity because ambiguity is our natural state.

> *Authenticity comes from a single faithfulness:*
> *that to the ambiguity of experience.*
> —JOHN BERGER

You write to do justice to the lives of your characters.

> *And art itself may be defined as a single-minded attempt to*
> *render the highest kind of justice to the visible universe.*
> —JOSEPH CONRAD

And the result of your impassioned efforts carries you back to anxiety. But every problem, you realize now, is also an opportunity.

You learn that fiction is:

Subversive
(It asks you to question everything you've believed.)

Disturbing
(Maybe your received values are wrong or need changing.)

Morally based
(On your own examined values.)

Sensual
(Exists in images, like dreams.)

Life-affirming
(Most crucially so when life seems not worth living.)

Particular, precise, exact, concrete
(Like dreams and memories.)

Nonjudgmental
(No victims or villains; you don't judge your characters.)

Inquisitive
(Asks why? And how?)

Subjective
(Objectivity is an illusion.)

Discovery
(Because you're writing about what you don't understand.)

A way of life
(You're a writer wherever you are. You're in search of material.)

A failure

(But maybe a glorious failure.)

A cumulative activity

(Everything you write today goes to everything you will ever write.)

Intuitive and illogical

(No discovery, no surprise.)

About people

(Even if those people come disguised as angels, gnomes, or cockroaches.)

John Gardner explains the fiction writer's process:

. . . *in his imagination, he sees made-up people doing things— sees them clearly—and in the act of wondering what they will do next he sees what they will do next, and all this he writes down in the best, most accurate words he can find, understanding even as he writes that he may have to find better words later, and that a change in the words may mean a sharpening or deepening of the vision, the fictive dream or vision becoming more and more lucid, until reality, by comparison, seems cold, tedious, and dead.*

Exercise 1:

They Did and They Didn't

I've just read a book called *101 Plots Used and Abused* by James N. Young, published in 1945, when it sold in hardcover for $1.25. Mr. Young, then the associate editor of *Collier's* magazine, which many of you will not remember, outlines 107 (not 101) plots that he calls "tired and tiresome." I'm not sure why this seemed like a profitable project to undertake, but Mr. Young obviously did. Maybe you can prove him wrong. Here's number 51: "Two old people—a man and a woman who had once, years before, been in love with each other—correspond, with a view to looking each other over and possibly marrying. The man is a widower; the woman is a widow. They make arrangements to meet somewhere—usually the lobby of some great hotel; and they describe each other. Each is to wear a distinguishing mark of some sort—a flower perhaps. But they never actually meet. Each manages to steal a peek at the other; and both sneak away—and, later, report that they had been unavoidably detained by something or other." Let's work with this. Write about these two, give them names and addresses in separate cities. Write about their youthful love affair and the eventual breakup. Summarize their years of separate marital bliss or suffering, whichever it was. Describe their disjoined lives until now. Maybe sample their recent correspondence. How did they hook up again anyway? Now give us the scene in the hotel lobby—describe the lobby using all of your senses. Let's suppose that they do, in fact, avoid each other as Young suggests. Let's follow them back to their homes and to their lives. Do they wonder what they may have just let slip through their hands? What now for each? Now let's turn the tables and suppose that they do meet and hit it off, and they marry and start a new life. Write about that new life. Is it happy? Maybe you play both scenarios out in the same novel—if you want to write this as your novel. You begin at that moment when she was going to walk away but turns once more to look at him and thinks . . . ? And feels . . . ? And . . . And then write two plots that you braid together, one in which they meet, one in which they do not, and follow their lives. What might have been.

Exercise 2:

Morality

You have to have a vision of the world to write a story or a novel and you have to be in touch with it. You always want to write from a moral position, which is not a message, but a passionate caring inside you. So write about your moral beliefs. What makes the world a better place to live? What makes it difficult? If not for you, then for others. Is there evil in the world? Can you identify it? What are your prejudices? Where do they come from? What keeps you up at night? (Or should.)

Exercise 3:

There and Then

Write about where you want to be right now. On a beach in the south of France. At the theater in London. In a cozy cottage on the Aran Isles. (Don't you wish!) Now go there and situate yourself in that place. Look around you. What's to your right? Your left? What's behind you? In front of you? Look down and then look above your head. Listen, inhale the air. Begin to write down the details of this place. Pretend that you're remembering the place from your last visit. Memory is imagination. Write in first person, present tense. The smell and the sounds and the textures. See yourself clearly. Are you sitting, standing, walking? Stop what you're doing and reach down and pick up the object at your feet. What is it? Describe it. Put it in your pocket or your pack. Whenever you see this object again, you'll remember this idyll, this wonderful trip to your favorite place. Write about the people who are there and the people who are not. Time to return. What does it feel like to leave?

Chapter Three

The Plot

Tell me a story!

No matter how luminous your prose or how fascinating your characters, if you have no plot—no narrative shape—if the characters have nothing meaningful to accomplish, the reader will put down your story. Plot is the gravity that holds the world of your story together. It's your weapon of suspense. Wield it wisely, and the reader will want to know what happens next.

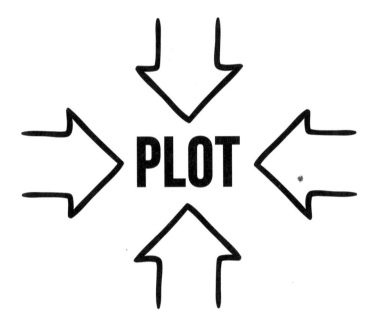

Aristotle said that a plot has a beginning, a middle, and an end. Plots proceed through a series of reversals and recognitions, A reversal (peripeteia) being a change in a situation to its opposite, a recognition (anagnorisis) being a change from ignorance to knowledge.

The basic plot of every story:

 You have a central character
—*Just 1!*

 Who wants something
—*Intensely*

 And goes after it
—*Must act! No passive central characters*

 Despite opposition
—*Conflict is at the heart of every story*

 And as a result of a struggle
—*It can't be easy*

 Comes to a win or a loss
—*The central character's problem is resolved, one way or the other*

The Central Character

You can only have one per plot. Not two. Not the oppressed minority. One person in trouble. The central character is a person even if he is not: Zeus, Dracula, Winnie-the-Pooh, Napoleon the Pig. Fiction is about people.

Give the central character a name we can't forget.

Anna Karenina	Humbert Humbert
Holden Caulfield	Quentin Compson
Atticus Finch	Sherlock Holmes
Binx Bolling	Huckleberry Finn
Frankie Machine	Milo Minderbinder
Uriah Heep	Robinson Crusoe
Tristram Shandy	Dorian Gray
Ichabod Crane	Jean Valjean

If you do this right, your central character will live longer than you will. Shakespeare is dead. Hamlet is alive, even though he dies each performance onstage.

What is an intriguing central character like?

Active
(you can't write a story
about a passive central
character)

Persistent

Not a victim or a villain

Flawed
(just like we are)

Has a rich interior life

**Takes responsibility for
her actions**

Where do I find these intriguing central characters?

In newspapers

On the bus

Sitting alone in restaurants

In church

At Home Depot

At the supermarket

Behind closed doors

In books

More thoughts on character:

Characters in fiction have aspirations and regrets; they have attitudes, memories, and secrets. They've had traumas in their lives. They have friends (never enough of them) and enemies (always too many). They hurt and they feel joy. They have senses of humor and wonder, which they cultivate or don't.

You're creating three-dimensional people, and you may not always like what they do, but you have to try to understand why they do it. Every man has his reasons, and the heart has reasons that reason cannot know. (Blaise Pascal said that.)

Your job is not to judge your characters but to witness what they do and to write that down. A character is what he does, what he means to do, what he thinks, and what he feels, but mostly he is what he does. We believe what we see, not what we're told. Actions, we know, speak louder than words. Put up or shut up, we tell the procrastinator. The proof is in the pudding. A picture is worth a thousand words, and all that. Love is a behavior, as we understand it, not an emotion or a platitude.

The characters are also like us in that they are not victims or villains. Some people may act villainously, and others may be victimized, but this behavior does not define them. What the characters in fiction are not—they are not passive. They want something intensely and they go after it.

Your central character must change by the end of the story. The change can be psychological or emotional, can be subtle or dramatic. As a result of his struggle, he has come to some understanding that he didn't have when he started his journey. And when you want us to see your character or when you want to see her, don't describe her, give her something to do.

Creating compelling and convincing characters whom the reader feels strongly about is the writer's most important job.

Write about people who have a lot at stake and a lot to lose. Make them want something intensely, let them go after it, and put obstacles in their way!

A character . . . has to be ignorant of the future, unsure about the past, and not at all sure of what he's supposed to be doing.

—Anthony Burgess

Character is the heart of fiction!

First: An invective against self-pity.

Self-pity is the least attractive quality in a central character (or anyone else, for that matter). A little of it goes a long way. Central characters don't whine. Self-pity is a license to do nothing. And we can't have a character who does nothing. Self-pity allows the character to see himself as a victim who has no control over his fate and can't change anything. Well, stories are all about change. Self-pity is humorless, self-indulgent, and unattractive. It is a refusal to understand and an act of cowardice.

> *Self-pity is easily the most destructive of the non-pharmaceutical narcotics; it is addictive, gives momentary pleasure and separates the victim from reality.*
> —JOHN GARDNER

Yes, as the Buddhists say, pain is inevitable, but suffering is optional.

> *Self-pity is our worst enemy and if we yield to it, we can never do anything good in this world.*
> —HELLEN KELLER

The Hero's Journey

Lord Raglan–Joseph Campbell

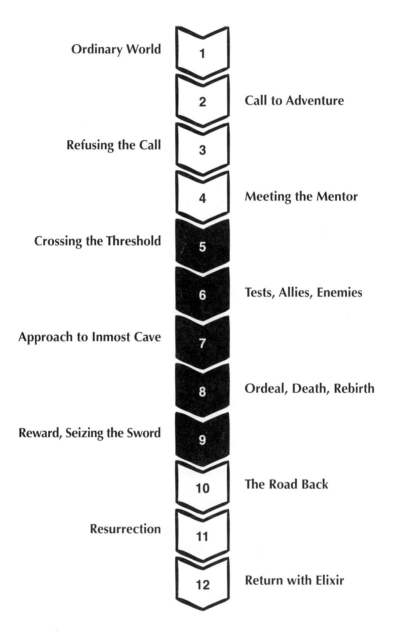

Ordinary World — 1

2 — Call to Adventure

Refusing the Call — 3

4 — Meeting the Mentor

Crossing the Threshold — 5

6 — Tests, Allies, Enemies

Approach to Inmost Cave — 7

8 — Ordeal, Death, Rebirth

Reward, Seizing the Sword — 9

10 — The Road Back

Resurrection — 11

12 — Return with Elixir

Your central character may take the hero's journey, and that journey will be the design of the plot. The scheme first appeared in Lord Raglan's *The Hero: A Study in Tradition, Myth and Drama* and was later used and altered by Joseph Campbell in *The Hero with a Thousand Faces*.

The Hero's Journey:

1. Hero introduced in his ordinary world where he receives

2. A call.

3. He is reluctant at first.

4. But is encouraged by a wise old man or woman to

5. Cross the first threshold

6. Where he encounters tests and helpers.

7. He reaches the innermost cave

8. Where he endures the supreme ordeal.

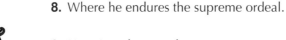

9. He seizes the sword or treasure,

10. And is pursued on the road home.

11. He's resurrected and transformed by the experience and

12. Returns to his ordinary world with treasure, boon, or elixir to benefit his world.

Wants something

The central character must want something intensely. It is the intensity that motivates the action. You also must know why your central character wants what he wants.

 Boy wants girl.
(Good so far.)

 Why? She's cute. He's lonely.

 Boy sits home waiting for girl to call.
(Whoops! No story!)

He didn't want her badly enough to knock on her door, call on her phone, not take no for answer, buy her flowers, sweet-talk her father, or make her a mixtape.

Goes after it

Goes after it right away—on page one if possible. Backstory can wait. No passive central characters. Only people who act are interesting. No couch potatoes need apply.

 Faulkner's advice:
Get your hero up a tree; throw rocks at her, and then get her down.

I would never write about someone who was not at the end of his rope.

–Stanley Elkin

If you're writing a story and are confused about the end, go back to the beginning.

–Cynthia Ozick

Beginnings

You want to begin your story when everything but the action is over. The first line is the line that breaks the silence, so it is your most important line and, perhaps, your most poetic. But you likely won't discover it in your first draft. It will more than likely appear in revision. You must catch the reader's attention immediately or there's no need to go on.

A good beginning is full of intimation and assurance:

 Intimation that here are characters who have something remarkable to tell us.

 Assurance that something compelling, surprising, unusual is about to happen.

A good first line:

Must take the reader out of her world and place her in the world of the story.

Must make the reader want to go on to the next sentence.

Charms, amazes, intrigues, shocks, or seduces.

Ought to present specific character, specific incident, specific conversation, specific mood.

Is intriguing, energetic, immediate, unqualified.

Has implicit in it the whole story.

Whatever you do, don't:

Promise what you can't deliver.

Initiate a conflict you won't resolve.

Load a gun you will not fire.

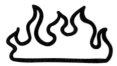

Light a fire you will not extinguish.

Begin with long descriptions or any description without establishing POV.

Begin with an idea.

Introduce a story; just jump in. Begin as close to the end as you can.

Start clean and simple. Don't try to write pretty or noble or big. Try to say just what you mean.

—William Sloane

Some people who began well:

All children, except one, grow up.
—*PETER PAN* BY J. M. BARRIE

A provocative character description. Intimations if immortality. Of course we'll read it.

The Jackmans' marriage had been adulterous and violent, but in its last days they became a couple again, as they might have if one of them were slowly dying.
—"THE WINTER FATHER" BY ANDRE DUBUS

A brilliantly ironic and tragic statement. We're most alive when we know we're dying. A theme worth exploring. Here's a writer who's taking a chance.

What to know about pain is how little we do to deserve it, how simple it is to give, how hard to lose.
—"WIDOW WATER" BY FREDERICK BUSCH

An eloquent statement of an important theme. We know we're in good hands when the narrator can be so clear about what is so complex.

As Gregor Samsa awoke one morning from uneasy dreams he found himself transformed in his bed into a gigantic insect.
—*THE METAMORPHOSIS* BY FRANZ KAFKA

How's the author going to pull this off? More importantly, what does it feel like to be a bug?

Francis Marion Tarwater's uncle had been dead for only half a day when the boy got too drunk to finish digging the grave and a Negro named Buford Munson, who had come to get a jug filled, had to finish it and drag the body from the breakfast table where it was still sitting and bury it in a decent Christian way, with the sign of its Savior at the head of the grave and enough dirt on top keep the dogs from digging it up.
—"YOU CAN'T BE ANY POORER THAN DEAD"
BY FLANNERY O'CONNOR

Humor, death, wantonness, religion, and a couple of beguiling characters–who could stop here?

It was the afternoon of my eighty-first birthday, and I was in bed with my catamite when Ali announced that the archbishop had come to see me.
—*EARTHLY POWERS* BY ANTHONY BURGESS

Certainly promise of intriguing characters here!

When I finally caught up with Abraham Trahearne, he was drinking beer with an alcoholic bulldog named Fireball Roberts in a ramshackle joint just outside of Sonoma, California, drinking the heart right out of a fine spring afternoon.
—*THE LAST GOOD KISS* BY JAMES CRUMLEY

We need to get to know that bulldog!

Many years later, as he faced the firing squad, Colonel Aureliano Buendía was to remember that distant afternoon when his father took him to discover ice.
—*ONE HUNDRED YEARS OF SOLITUDE*
BY GABRIEL GARCÍA MÁRQUEZ

Death and treachery, discovery and family, present and past. We'll read on.

Despite opposition

Conflict is at the heart of every story. Only trouble is interesting. What is stopping the central character from getting what she wants?

Writing a story is taking the path of most resistance.

Everything that you don't want to happen to yourself or to your family or friends, should happen to your characters!

And as a result of a struggle

It can't be easy. She must try and try. (And if at first you succeed, try, try again.)

Make the struggle difficult. Make it seemingly impossible for your central character to get what she wants. The opposition must be formidable and worthy.

You can't change plots in midstream. If it's a story about a woman trying to save her marriage, she can't run off with the pool boy at the first sign of difficulty. That would be a different story.

Comes to a win or a loss

The story and the central character's struggle must be resolved, and the central character must be changed as a result of her own actions.

We don't need the resolution of the character's life, just of the character's problem.

The seven words you cannot use to end your story: "And they all lived happily ever after." Why? Because none of us do live ever after (the first lie) and so there goes the happy part, too (the second).

Motiveless Activity and the Early Flashback

Begin with scene if you can, but don't begin with some motiveless activity in scene and then launch into a flashback. Like this:

> *"Jeff drove his PT Cruiser into the Pollo Tropical parking lot and listened to the end of the Stones' 'Sympathy for the Devil.' He noticed the attractive young couple in the VW Beetle. He remembered when he and Ellen went to the junior prom in his Bug: 'Do you think we'll make it?' Ellen had said."*

If you have a flashback on the first page of your story, reconsider. Here's why. One or two things may have happened. First, you wrote your few sentences and realized that you didn't know enough about your character to continue. And so you wrote some backstory—the night of the prom, in this case. You wrote until you were comfortable that you knew your character a little better, and then you returned to the parking lot. Well, you needed to write that backstory, but we don't need to read it. Your plot, the character's struggle, must happen in the present of the story, not in the past. Cut the flashback. The second possibility is that you found your real material. You began the story in the parking lot just to get your character doing something, just to get the narrative under way. You didn't really know why he was at Pollo Tropical. Hunger, perhaps. He's acting without purpose, we might say. And then you found that the real trouble is in the past, back there with Ellen, back in high school. The love of his life, the woman he lost. Well, now what you need to do is jettison the opening and get us back into the past. (Which becomes the present of the story.) In his wonderful book on writing, *The Triggering Town*, Richard Hugo says there are always two subjects, the triggering subject (in this case, the parking lot, the song, the VW Beetle) and the generated subject (Ellen and the prom). The generated subject is the one with the emotional intensity needed to carry you, your characters, and your reader through the story.

And in the end . . .

 Don't end the story with a thought, an idea, or a spoken word if you can. Leave us with a compelling visual image of the central character, one so resonant that it stays with us when we close the book! A freeze-frame.

A few guidelines for endings:

 May finish lyrically—you've earned the right to soar.

Shouldn't be loose, drift off, or dissolve.

 Can be dramatic or muted (the story has made its point or has failed).

Should not be a trick or a gimmick.

Should not remind us about what happened.

 Does not introduce new information.

Must resolve what's gone before it.

 Should be inherent in the opening.

Does not deliver a moral or a lesson.

 Can't bail the story out.

No deus ex machina.

Some people who ended well:

So we beat on, boats against the current,
borne back ceaselessly into the past.
—THE GREAT GATSBY BY F. SCOTT FITZGERALD

Haunting, unforgettable, and profound.
The past is the gravity we cannot escape.

Don't ever tell anybody anything. If you do, you start missing everybody.
—THE CATCHER IN THE RYE BY J.D. SALINGER

Talking about your pain does not lessen it. Why does everything
we love vanish? Why does every touch leave a bruise?

. . . and then he asked me would I yes to say yes my mountain
flower and first I put my arms around him yes and drew him down
to me so he could feel my breasts all perfume yes and his heart
was going like mad and yes I said yes I will Yes.
—ULYSSES BY JAMES JOYCE

How the emotions soar as the novel tries to end. The
indomitable Molly Bloom carries us away.

But I reckon I got to light out for the Territory ahead of
the rest, because Aunt Sally she's going to adopt me and sivilize
me and I can't stand it. I been there before.
—THE ADVENTURES OF HUCKLEBERRY FINN BY MARK TWAIN

Freedom trumps civilization. Adventure trumps certainty.
Huck's about to reinvent himself.

Motivations in collision

Plot is the central character's problem and the struggle to solve it.

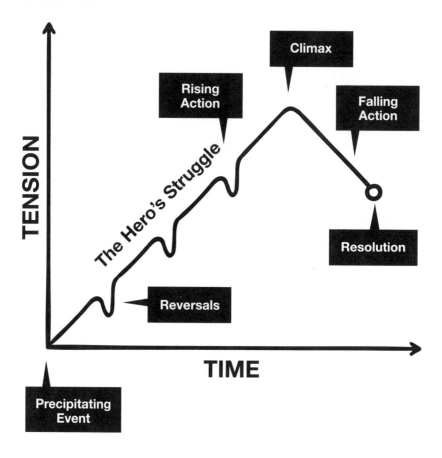

TENSION

The Hero's Struggle

Reversals

Rising Action

Climax

Falling Action

Resolution

TIME

Precipitating Event

Plot is the architecture of action. But life doesn't come with plots, you say. (Except for the one they bury us in.) Life is just one thing after another, you say, and you're right. Here's the difference between life and fiction:

Fiction has to make sense!

Storyville!

Story versus plot

According to E. M. Forster, "The king died and then the queen died" is a story. "The king died and then the queen died of grief" is a plot.

Story: Chronology

Plot: Causality

According to Anthony Lane, the Quentin Tarantino plot goes something like this: "The king died while having sex on the hood of a lime-green Corvette, and the queen died of contaminated crack borrowed from the court jester, with whom she was enjoying a conversation about the relative merits of Tab and Diet Pepsi as they sat and surveyed the bleeding remains of the lords and ladies whom she had just blown away with a stolen .45 in a fit of grief."

Story: Asks the question "What?"

Plot: Asks "Why?"

The problem of narration is not . . . the problem of "finding
the words," but that of choosing and placing events, of allowing
or instigating their wordless dialogue.
—JOHN BERGER

If immoral works of literature exist, they are
works in which there is no plot.
—CESAR PAVESE

Story: Is about the conjunction "And . . ."

Plot: Is about the conjunction "So . . ."

Post hoc ergo propter hoc

This is a logical fallacy (often shortened to the post hoc fallacy) in philosophy, meaning "after this, therefore, because of this." In other words because A precedes B it must be the cause of it. However, because your character cut himself shaving in the first scene of the story does not necessarily mean that the nick caused the death of his father in the second act. The death of one person is not the consequence of the injury to another.

The fallacy is also known as false cause or coincidental correlation or correlation not causation. The danger for the fiction writer is that she mistakes chronology for causality. Just because one incident in the story precedes another does not make it a cause. And, of course, we want a causal relationship between events in a plot. In a pharmaceutical context we can see the error at work in statements attributing heroin use to pot smoking. Yes, many heroin addicts smoked pot first, but many more of them drank milk first. Because the rooster crows before the sun rises does not mean the rooster causes the sun to rise. Unless you're into magical thinking.

Plot: A completed process of change

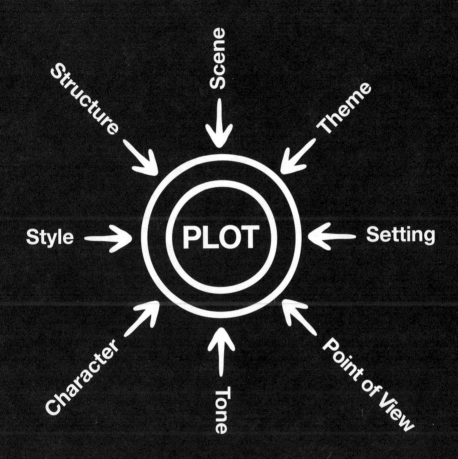

Plot is the gravitational force
that holds the expanding universe
of your story together.

Plot is character revealed by action.

—Aristotle

We can perhaps reduce all stories to these two plots:

A stranger rides into town.

A person sets off on a quest.

We have plots because we insist on meaning. Yes, life is stranger than fiction. Because, as mentioned earlier, fiction has to make sense! (And if life made sense we wouldn't need stories.)

A plot begins to take shape when you begin to ask the appropriate narrative questions:

+ What does my central character want?

+ Why does she want it?

+ What's stopping her from getting it? Or who is?

+ What does she do about the obstacles in her way?

+ What are the results of what she does?

+ What climax does this struggle lead to?

+ Does she get what she wants in the end?

+ How does that make her feel?

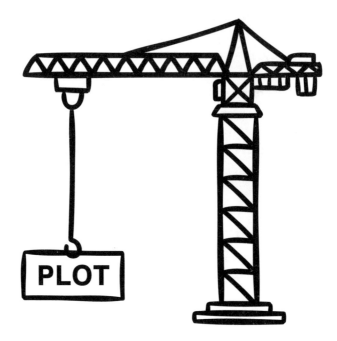

According to John Gardner there are three ways to construct a plot:

First, you have a situation and you muddle ahead to a resolution. These are the stories that begin with a compelling situation, a husband leaving a wife, say, or with an interesting character. You begin by letting the central character want something enough to go after it. Ernest J. Gaines says that all stories should begin with a man in the middle of the Santa Monica Freeway at rush hour. He moves or the story's over. Then you follow him around with your pen and paper as Faulkner followed Caddy Compson.

Second, you have an event, a climactic one normally, and you imagine what led up to it. These kinds of situations appear in the newspaper every day and are the regular subject of gossip in bars and on telephones. You just need to stay alert. Did you hear that he's leaving her after twenty-five years of marriage? For some little hussy. Now you think, *What was going on in that home, at the office, in his head, that led to that decision?*

Third, you borrow the plot. That's what Shakespeare did. They're just there to give the characters something to do anyway.

We'll add one more method: You take the plot from your own life.

1. Muddling ahead

A husband tells his wife he's going to leave her.

She's the central character. You'll call her Ruth. Call him Kenneth.

She wants to save the marriage because she loves him to death.

She pleads with him to stay. He does not.

She goes to his place of business and tries to convince him to come home. He does not.

She convinces him to go to marriage counseling. It does not go as she had planned.

And so on. Every time Ruth tries to win Kenneth back, she drives him further away.

The plot must be resolved. She'll win or she'll lose. You'll find out.

2. Back to square one

You get your climactic event from a headline in the newspaper, perhaps. This one, let's say: "Intoxicated Woman on Stolen Horse Tries to Rob Convenience Store."

INTOXICATED WOMAN ON STOLEN HORSE TRIES TO ROB CONVENIENCE STORE

Well, what led up to that?

We're in rural Alabama (because that's where the real event happened). Let's call our town Coushatta. Sissy had a four-pronged turkey lifter down her pants when Glink Babcock, night manager at the Li'l General, tapped her on the shoulder.

Sissy tied the horse up to the ice machine outside the store. She had tied a plastic bag of Keystone Lights to the saddle horn. She took a pull out of the near-empty can, dropped the can to the ground, and stomped it flat with her boot. She burped.

She got the horse, Buttercup, a blue-eyed splashed white mare, at her neighbor Jimmy Harris's ranch where it was tied to a hitching post outside the barn. Jimmy would never press charges. She knows too much about his secret life.

When her date for the evening, Warren Steele, fell asleep on the couch, she went through his wallet and pockets but found no money. No money, no loving. She did find a photo of the little jezebel Tracylee Hall. With her phone number written on the back. Son of a bitch will pay for this.

 Warren showed up at Sissy's single-wide after his double shift at the water treatment plant over in the county seat. He smelled so bad he'd knock a buzzard off a honey wagon.

 Sissy made a cheesy tuna noodle bake in anticipation of Warren's visit and prepared two Sunny D screwdrivers for the festivities. Said festivities would ensue just as soon as Warren showered down. She was making it up to him for her unwarranted jealousy.

 And we can take this trouble back to the dance at Jordi's Blue Light on Friday last when Sissy saw Warren's cheating eyes follow Tracylee's ample caboose across the dance floor and she told him you're mine or you're no one's.

3. Borrowing the plot

What you'll do is take a Shakespearean play or a work of classical literature or folklore and base your story on that. Only you will change the time and the place and the characters. What you'll end up with is your own plot, but with allusions to a classical work. The way, say, *West Side Story* is not *Romeo and Juliet*, but certainly owes a debt to the play. Here are two I did quickly.

The Glass of Fashion (*Hamlet*):

 After learning that his father's murderer might be his uncle, an acting student determines to learn the truth, and, if Uncle is guilty, to murder him, before the student is murdered himself by his uncle's henchmen.

 The boss of Manhattan's Mastrovito crime family, Aldo the Cat Mastrovito, is gunned down at the Due Amici Ristorante during the San Giovanni Festival. Rumor has it that the hit was ordered by Aldo's own brother and capo, Nicky Slacks.

 Nicky had already seduced Aldo's wife Allesandra on a recent Vegas holiday and may have been worried that Aldo would find out.

 Nicky's the natural replacement for his brother as the new don.

No sooner does he take over when he has the actual triggermen executed and marries his brother's widow. Eyebrows are raised, but tongues are silent.

 Aldo's boy Gianni is upset with his mother for disrespecting his father by marrying so soon. He calls Nicky "Uncle Dad." Nicky's not happy.

Gianni receives a package containing his father's ear and an anonymous note fingering Nicky as having ordered the killing. Gianni's not sure he believes it, but he'll find out.

He's an acting student at the New York Conservatory. He knows this will be the performance of his life, convincing his uncle that he's daft and harmless while he plots his revenge.

Nicky's not taking chances and has several of his men spying on Gianni.

Gianni turns on his girlfriend Annette, the daughter of Nicky's right-hand man. Their relationship deteriorates and he allows it to. She grows distraught.

A year has passed and he has had several opportunities to kill his uncle but he has hesitated. Was he lied to? Did he have proof? He has lost the rage he once felt and needs it restored.

He writes a script for the small acting company and invites his mother and uncle to the premiere. The play is about the murder of a mafia don.

And so on . . . Annette, depressed, kills herself. Gianni mistakes her father for Nicky and kills him. Nicky realizes now what's going on and he wants his nephew killed, but needs it done discreetly so as not to upset his wife overmuch. He hires a couple of Gianni's actor friends to take Gianni for a ride and kill him. But Gianni turns the trick and has them killed by a rival mob. Annette's brother Paulie hears of her death and goes after Gianni. They all die.

3. Borrowing the plot (continued)

O My Name It Is Nothing (*The Odyssey*)

 The war in Afghanistan is over for Captain Jimmy Kaltsis. All he has to do now is escape his Taliban captors and make his way home.

 Captain Jimmy Kaltsis, career soldier, is on his final deployment when he and five of his men are captured by Taliban forces and taken to an undisclosed location in the eastern mountains.

 Jimmy's son, an Army Ranger stationed at Fort Kabul, learns of his father's plight when he sees a video of the prisoners captured by the Taliban. He vows to rescue his dad even if he has to go AWOL.

 Meanwhile, Jimmy and his men seize an opportunity and escape their captors after a bloody skirmish.

 They head into the mountains in a commandeered Humvee, finding shelter in a remote and idyllic village apparently unaffected by the war. His wounded men are looked after by the villagers.

 The men fall into the habit of smoking opium with the locals and decide they never want to leave.

 Jimmy sets off on foot for the Pakistani border on his own, promising to return with help.

 After several firefights, Jimmy is wounded and exhausted. He's rescued by a woman, who takes him to her hut. She has a young child. Her husband is off at war.

She nurses Jimmy to health. The three of them make an instant family. Jimmy and the woman become romantically involved.

Meanwhile, his son has left camp, gone native, and is in pursuit of his dad. The son, half Pakistani himself, speaks Pashto and Dari. He knows the Army is on his trail as a deserter.

He makes it to the idyllic village and learns from the wasted soldiers where his dad was headed. He follows with a guide.

The son arrives at the woman's hut not long after Jimmy has left.

She tells the son that Jimmy is headed for Peshawar, but will have to pass through Taliban territory to get there.

When Jimmy is caught in an ambush by Taliban soldiers, his son comes to the rescue, but Jimmy doesn't recognize who he is, as he fires down from the mountain above.

4. This is my life

You take the plot from your own life. You'll alter things, perhaps, to make them more dramatic. You are after the truth, not the facts. Every life is interesting; every life dramatic. Write about yourself when you are most yourself—in love with things that vanish. Write about what happened (fact) and then write about what didn't happen (truth).

 On your way home from school on the bus, your friend Bob tells you that Kathleen O is in love with you but is too shy to say anything.

 You never thought of dating Kathleen, though you have admired her from a distance. You can't sleep.

 You can't get Kathleen out of your mind. You imagine the two of you on a cruise to Bimini, at the breakfast table in your new house, at the wedding of your eldest daughter.

 You have fallen in love with Kathleen.

At school in the morning, you seek her out.

 You find her with Raymond D.

Bob's pronouncement yesterday was an erroneous supposition. She is not in love with you, but with Raymond.

There are certain benefits of taking your material from life:

You know the setting.

You recall incidents that will become scenes.

You have characters that you know, or think you know (and that may amount to the same thing in fiction).

You have a beginning, a middle, and an end.

So it should be easy, right? Wrong. The benefits are also the disadvantages.

The disadvantages:

You don't really know the characters, not even yourself.

+ The character in the story is not the model you based him on.

You might be tempted to be slavish to facts and the trivia.

+ Trivia may intrude in life, but should not in fiction.

+ The reader won't care that it happened that way, that the phone rang at a dramatic moment. Get rid of the phone.

So remember:

Invention is inevitable.

Don't be slavish to "what really happened" (fiction is telling the truth, not the facts).

Forget your models and attend to the characters.

Memory

Memory's first job is to keep us alive. The saber-toothed tigers live on the plains, my friend, so let's stay in the forest. Or, The last time I ate an oyster, I became deathly ill. I'll have the smoked mullet tonight.

Memory can be false. Just ask any two people to remember a dinner and conversation they shared or an accident they witnessed. One of the versions must be inaccurate. Probably both are.

Memory, like dreaming, and like imagining, forms a mental image of what is not actually present. Memory, then, is a creative act like writing a story is a creative act. Memory is reproductive imagination. It is the past re-created and distilled. We remember the gist of the event: all that was vivid and consequential.

Once you begin to examine your past, you'll see that your life opens up to you. One memory leads to the next. You only need to attend to the memories and to your ensuing emotional responses to have all the material you'll ever need.

The two best pieces of writing advice you will ever get:

 Finish the story!

 Don't think you're going to finish it today, or in this draft, or any time in the near future.

If you don't learn to finish, you can't learn to write.

Story as iceberg

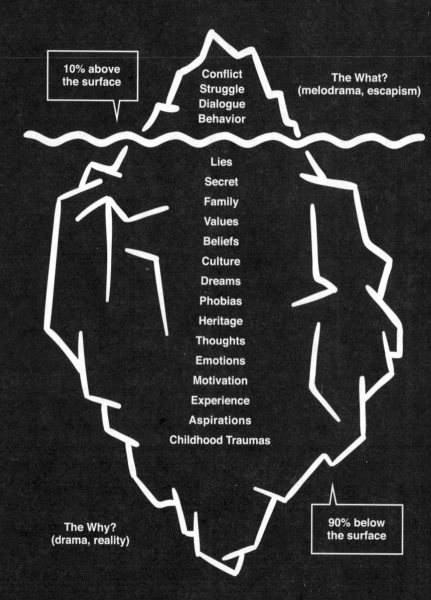

10% above
the surface

Conflict
Struggle
Dialogue
Behavior

The What?
(melodrama, escapism)

Lies
Secret
Family
Values
Beliefs
Culture
Dreams
Phobias
Heritage
Thoughts
Emotions
Motivation
Experience
Aspirations
Childhood Traumas

The Why?
(drama, reality)

90% below
the surface

**A story asks the question why and dives
beneath the surface for the answer.**

The shape of things to come

You take the definition of plot that we talked about and let the plot do your thinking for you. It will lead you, quite naturally, to considerations of setting, theme, characterization, point of view, voice, and so on. Don't resist it; use it to your advantage.

You have to come up with a chronological sequence for your actions, a time frame for your novel, even if you choose not to tell the story chronologically. Plot, E. M. Forster wrote, is an organism of a higher type (than story), and it is also a narration of events, the emphasis this time falling on causality. In a story, we ask, "And then what?" In a plot, we ask, "Why?" So maybe we can say this: The plot is the form that the causal sequence of events assumes, and the narrative structure is the shape of the entire utterance, the whole story. Plot is the force that drives through the story.

Every force evolves a form.
—MOTHER ANN LEE

Narrative structure is the matrix in which the plot is nurtured and developed. Plot is the causal shape of the story or novel; narrative structure is the chronological and the architectural.

I saw the angel in the marble and carved until I set him free.
—MICHELANGELO

Thinking about the plot

You can think of your plot like this. Your status quo is disrupted by an event that results in a new status quo. The example here is from the novel *Louisiana Power & Light*:

Situation: Billy Wayne wants to be a priest.
Complication: He meets Earlene.
Result: He marries Earlene.

Which causes:

Situation: Billy Wayne regrets his decision.
Complication: Billy Wayne meets Tammy Lynne.
Result: He has an affair with Tammy Lynne.

Which causes:

Situation: Billy Wayne regrets this dalliance.
Complication: He realizes his marriage is in trouble.
Result: He confesses to Earlene.

Which causes Earlene to leave him, and so on.

Or think of the rhythm of the plot as problem-solution-problem-solution, etc. The example here from "Hansel and Gretel":

Problem: Parents are poor.
Solution: Get rid of the children.
Problem: Children don't want to leave.
Solution: Take them for a long walk in the woods.
Problem: Children are abandoned, lost.
Solution: Rescued by a little old lady.
Problem: The lady is a child-eating witch.

And so on . . .

Every story is a clock, a calendar, and a time machine

So let's try using a metaphor as a structure for our story. We'll write about classical musicians by using the shape of a musical form. If we were going to write a novel, we might choose the symphony form. And already we would have our shape: the book would be divided into the four sections of the classical symphony: allegro, andante, scherzo, rondo. But we're going to write a short story, so we'll stick with the sonata (song) form that's used in some symphonic movements. We'll let the form and the plot lead us. We won't hesitate to change the form if that helps us get the story told. We'll do an outline here, which we know we'll revise. But it will get us started. Our working title is *Double Sonata*. Our central character is Theo Stanton, a cellist, who is head-over-heels in love with the new woman in the chamber orchestra, Phoebe White. He wants her. He goes after her. The story is divided into the three sections of the sonata form: exposition, development, and recapitulation, and we might, perhaps, add the optional coda and intro. And this is what we know before we start: whatever else the story is about, it is about passionate love and sublime music.

SONATA FORM

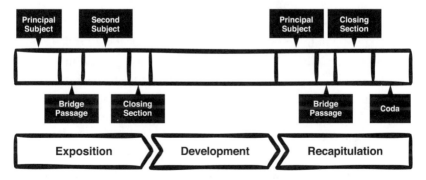

The intro will be quick. We set the scene: a spacious rehearsal hall where the musicians in our chamber orchestra are assembling. They settle into their chairs, unpack their instruments, arrange the sheet music on their stands, and wait for the oboist to play her clear and penetrating A note. And as they are waiting, we begin with Act I in which we introduce our principal character and a principal theme. The opening act's tempo is fairly fast—allegro—but more dignified, really, than hurried. Theo's in his chair wiping the strings of his cello with a soft cloth. He can't wait to begin playing, to find himself enveloped in glorious melody. Maybe he has a cold. He's not looking or feeling his best. His eyes are itchy. His nose is red and drippy. He's wearing a scarf and his *Let's Get Bizet* T-shirt. He's hot; he's cold. His ears are blocked. (Okay, we've humanized him enough.) And now a bridge passage to our second subject. As the musicians tune to the oboe, Theo can faintly hear that one of the bassoons is flat.

And now we'll introduce our second principal character and a second principal theme. The conductor, Maestro Tonelli, enters the hall with the newest member of the orchestra. He introduces Phoebe to her colleagues, who clap politely. She smiles and bows. Her eyes are Egyptian blue; her hair short, spiky, and flaxen. Theo is struck by her beauty: the high cheekbones, the long neck, the slightly celestial nose. She looks like one of Modigliani's young women. (Okay, we've angelicized her enough.) He can't take his inflamed eyes off her. Beauty this radiant, this hypnotic, would be too painful to live without, he thinks. It is as if he'd been struck by lightning. It would have been better never to have seen her than to have her in the world apart from him—that could only lead to despair. He has to have her. He'll go after her now, we can be sure. (And if we think this stroke of lightning, this love at first sight, is all a little too over the top, we'll dial it back in revision.)

Phoebe plays the mandolin, of all things. She takes off her sweater and Theo sees the hibiscus flower tattoo running up her right arm. The maestro asks her to play Beethoven's Sonatina in C Major for Mandolin and Piano. She shakes hands with Taylor George, the pianist, and sits. And for four minutes, Theo is transported. Her technique is flawless. Her playing is charismatic and energetic; she's got speed, tone, and imagination to burn. After the rehearsal, Theo waits for an opportunity to catch Phoebe alone, but the maestro chaperones her every move. Finally, Theo manages a handshake and greeting and asks Phoebe if she'd like to grab a coffee at the café across the street. He fibs and says it's allergies, not a cold; he's not contagious. Phoebe thanks him but says she needs to run. Theo tells her how much he enjoyed her playing. In a codetta to the opening act, we see Theo at home on the computer Googling Phoebe. He's surprised to learn that she is also in a bluegrass band, the Sawgrass Rangers, and they're playing tomorrow night at an outdoor venue in Fort Lauderdale. His mother calls to invite him for supper. He lies and tells her he'd love to but he's composing. She says, Like Mozart? He says no, Mozart's in his grave decomposing. This is one of their running jokes. And maybe it strikes you here that a story's plot has the same three-act structure as a joke—setup, buildup, payoff.

The tempo slows to andante in Act II, the development. Here is where the action happens. Here's where Theo struggles against all the obstacles we put in his way to win the hand and heart of Phoebe. We next see Theo at the bluegrass venue, and he's here to get Phoebe's attention and begin his courtship. He has to battle against his inherent shyness and his agonizing doubts. He's always behaved awkwardly in romantic situations. And let's face it, he's not grotesque or unsightly or anything, but he's no movie star, either. Why would this goddess go out with him? The band's opening set is a wonder. Close your eyes and it's Bill Monroe you're hearing. And Phoebe sings the high lonesome lyrics like she was to the bluegrass manner born. He wonders if she can see him in the second row. When she nods to someone she does see, Theo turns, and there's Taylor George, the man with two first names and long, flat, lean fingers, clapping his hands over his head. Damn! After the show, Theo sees Phoebe with Taylor, but approaches her anyway. Before he can ask her to go out for a drink, she invites him to join her and Taylor at Blue Martini for a nightcap. He's crestfallen. He's been outmaneuvered by Taylor before he even had a chance. He declines as graciously as he can. She says she'll take a rain check, and his heart leaps.

He can't sleep. He downloads the Sawgrass Rangers CD and listens to Phoebe's exquisite playing and her haunting vocal on "In the Pines."

Al Mesale, the tympanist, who lives on the third floor of the condo, stops by for coffee in the morning. They get to talking, and Al tells Theo that he heard the first violinist telling Mary Pat, the French horn player, that Phoebe had eyes for Theo. Theo is, at first, incredulous, but allows himself to believe in this miracle. He is newly emboldened. He memorizes what he'll say to Phoebe. At the next rehearsal Theo is waiting for Phoebe when Al comes over and apologizes. It wasn't Theo, after all, that Phoebe had eyes for. He misunderstood. It was Taylor. Theo will not be discouraged, however. Now he's desperate. He needs to ask her out immediately. The longer she sees Taylor, the harder it will be to woo her away. He meets her at the door and asks her out for dinner and a movie. She's taken aback. She tells him she's seeing Taylor tonight.

—Tomorrow, then.
—A gig.
—The day after.
—Okay, but I'm a vegan.
—We'll go to Sublime.
—No, the owner supported Mr. Tangerine Man in the presidential election. I'd rather eat a bucket of pork skins and a side of foie gras than eat there.
—Netflix and chill at my place, then. *Russian Ark*. Sweet potato and black bean veggie burgers.

And so the courtship begins. We see them having fun. Riding the water taxi, swimming at the beach, kayaking the New River, playing duets for mandolin and cello together at her place. They're writing a song together, "A Wild Night and a New Road." They're falling in love over music. When she's not playing, he stays at her place. He's given up meat. His mother thinks that's just insane. Phoebe's bluegrass career is taking off. The Sawgrass Rangers are about to embark on an extended tour of the South. She gives her notice at the orchestra. Theo and she see less and less of each other. When she's in town, she's practicing eight hours a day. Theo understands that practice goes with the territory, but that doesn't make him feel any better about it. His own playing is suffering and the maestro has noticed. He can't concentrate. He can't sleep.

They are out to dinner. Phoebe asks Theo if he dislikes the kale and quinoa salad. He's hardly touched it. He says, Where is this going?

—This?
—Us.
—We're in love, aren't we?
—But we're not headed anywhere.
—I like it as it is. The high intensity, the passion. Absence makes the heart grow fonder and all that.
—Not my heart. I think you care more for your music than you do for me.
—This is my career we're talking about. This is my dream. Aren't you happy for me?

And so the quarrel escalates and it ends with Theo saying, Maybe we should call the whole thing off. And her saying, If that's what you want, and him saying, That's it? That's all you have to say? And so ends our second act. Theo is despondent. But we know that he can't give up trying to win Phoebe's heart or we have no story. We're doing our job—making it hard for Theo to get what he wants.

And so begins our third act, the up-tempo recapitulation, in which we reintroduce our principal themes, music and love. After dinner Theo plays the song he wrote with Phoebe for his mother. She's rapt by the music, and he's carried away. He knows what he must do. He thanks his mother for the lovely brisket—he's eating meat again—and tells her he has something important to do right away. He rushes to Phoebe's condo and tells her he's calling the separation off. He can't live without her. He's miserable, he tells her. He's been dating a brass player. Nothing serious, of course. He'll do whatever Phoebe wants. He'll quit the orchestra and be her roadie. He just wants to be with her. Yes, he wants a deeper commitment from her, but he can live without it. We can work this out. When she can finally get a word in edgewise, she tells him that she's been seeing Taylor, and they've gotten serious.

—How serious?
—We're engaged.

—You love me and you know it.

—You walked away from love.

—And I'm back.

We wonder what they'll do, and in wondering, we'll learn what they do, and we'll write it down. Phoebe marries Taylor? Theo and Phoebe elope? (We hope.) And we still have the coda to write. Here it is: A peek into Theo's future:

A. Theo and Phoebe play a duet in their new home as their sweet little baby sleeps in the crib.

B. Phoebe and Theo huddle in a corner booth at Michael's in Miami on one of their clandestine trysts. Taylor's in Boston auditioning for the Boston Symphony.

C. Phoebe leaves Taylor at the altar and runs off with Theo.

Theo wins or Theo loses. Plot's resolved.

And now we have a rough outline of our story, but we realize we'll want to know a bit more about music if we're going to write about classical and popular musicians. We'll need to know how much time and effort goes into producing a CD, for example. We'll need to furnish Theo's Las Olas apartment and Phoebe's studio on the beach. And what is life like for a touring band? But we'll do all the research as we write and we'll have a blast creating this brave new world that has such marvelous creatures in it. And we want to give the maestro and Al more to do. And what about the members of Sawgrass Rangers? We'll need to get to know them.

Sit your ass in the chair

That's the first commandment of fiction writing. Writing is a physical activity. You're at your writing desk, but your central character's at the end of his rope. A desperate man taking desperate measures. Only trouble is interesting, and everything you don't want to happen to yourself or to your family and friends should happen to your hero. You love this man, but you keep putting obstacles in his way. Writing a story is taking the path of most resistance. So you dip your pen in the ink, and you begin at the edge of the cliff.

You sit at the desk and try to express the inexpressible. This makes you anxious. All stories are failures, but you know that a writer is the one not stopped or even fazed by failure. This makes you fearless. You don't know where the story's going, but you trust in the writing process and your imagination to get you there. You write about what you don't understand. What you don't know is more important than what you know because what you don't know engages your sense of wonder. You insist on meaning, but not on answers. As we've said, the point is not to answer, but to question; not to solve, but to seek; not to preach, but to explore. And you believe that life is stranger than fiction because fiction has to make sense.

This was said earlier but bears repeating. No matter how luminous your prose and how fascinating your characters, if you have no plot—no narrative shape—if the characters have nothing meaningful to accomplish, the reader will put down your story. And as we've said, the basic plot of every story is this: a central character wants something intensely, goes after it despite opposition, and as a result of a struggle comes to a win or a loss. You take this definition as a starting point and let the necessary plot do your thinking for you. The plot leads and you follow. Like this:

We begin, let's say, on Christmas Eve with sixty-nine-year-old Vivien, wife, mother, and grandmother, in the combination living room/dining room/kitchen of the one-bedroom, one-bath condo she shares with her husband on Hollywood Beach. And let's say we've decided to adhere to the classical unities of action, place, and time. Our story will focus on one action without subplots, will take place entirely on Christmas Eve, and entirely in this modest condo.

It's their forty-ninth Christmas together, their fourteenth in Florida. Vivien is setting the table for two with the holiday dishes, the cloth napkins, the good flatware. She arranges sprigs of plastic holly around the Santa candle. She sits a minute, smooths the wrinkles on the snowflake tablecloth, and recalls the Christmas when she was seventeen and in love with Patsy Fantasia, a boy with black curls, amber skin, and alarming blue eyes. She remembers the Christmas night he walked her home from midnight Mass in the snow. On her porch, he gave her a gift, a green box of Jean Naté body powder, took off his hat, and kissed her. She's fallen for it again, this annual trick the holidays perform of making *now* disappear and pulling *then* out of thin air. She wonders where Patsy is now, and does he ever think about her. Well, we've discovered a theme, haven't we? Time, the past and the present, mutability, lost love. Make that themes. Discovered by simply asking ourselves what was on Vivien's mind.

At twenty-one, she married Jackie Paradise. Jackie's asleep, sitting up on the sofa. She goes to him and brushes his gray hair with her fingers, says, "Jackie, where have you gone?" And we realize we have uncovered our requisite trouble, and it's big trouble: dementia—the loss of self, the loss of spouse, the beginning of the end of everything. Jackie swats at her hand and opens his eyes. Vivien can tell he doesn't know where he is. Does he know who she is? She says—

In writing a story, we have two choices: We write scene or summary. We show or tell. Scene reveals; summary explains. Scene is intimate and vivid; summary, distant and efficient. Scene is where the writer engages the imagination and the emotions of the reader. Everything important in a story should be shown, and this delicate moment between Vivien and Jackie is certainly that. It's the moment our plot gets under way.

Before we can write the opening scene, we'll need to look closer at the stage we've begun to set, at Vivien and Jackie in their multipurpose room, because when people speak, they also do things. And every detail in the room will tell us about the people who live here. Writing a story is archaeology. Not all the details in our notes will make it to the page, but, more importantly, each will afford us invaluable insight into our characters. The details that do make the page will be those that are eloquent and consequential. So we look around. The first thing we notice is an alarm on the front door. There's a milk-glass mixing bowl on the console table, and in the bowl are a watch, a Medic Alert card, and a wallet. The cloudy water in the small aquarium is empty of fish. There are three framed photographs on the wall and beneath each an explanatory Post-it note: "Your grandparents' wedding"; "Your family at the 1967 reunion"; "the lake house." There's a laptop computer on a TV tray by the La-Z-Boy and a flat-screen TV on the wall beside a bookcase. On the bookcase is a stuffed tabby cat—a grandchild's toy, perhaps?—and a shadow box with mementos of a vacation trip to London. The fluorescent light over the sink flickers. The motor to the fridge kicks on. Vivien has set out ribbon candy and Christmas cards on the card table, hung a wreath on the door, an Advent calendar on the fridge, and arranged a crèche on the buffet. The Magi are chipped but serviceable. When she looks at the figurines, she sees wisdom paying homage to innocence, logic to faith. Maybe faith is hope, she thinks. And we think she doesn't just want to care for Jackie, she wants to heal him.

Jackie's wearing the reindeer sweater that Vivien knitted for him and the gray jogging pants—that's what she calls them—really just shabby thrift-store sweatpants, but she doesn't want to think he's just given up on being presentable. The right word can make all the difference. The sleeves of the sweater are pushed up to his elbows. It's warm in the house. The small finger of his left hand is bent with arthritis. He has a faded tattoo of a compass rose on his left forearm. Vivien's had her gray hair done, short with long layers. She's wearing a fuchsia knit polo dress with a ribbed black shirt collar and black sleeve bands and black ballerina slippers. When she catches a glimpse of herself in the wall mirror, she likes what she sees; she's looking good, if she doesn't mind saying so herself. She's got a discreet hearing aid in her left ear and a half-inch scar above her right eye. We know that every scar tells a story, but will this particular story be relevant to our story? We'll find out. She wears a silver crucifix ring that belonged to her mom. We decide it's her most precious possession. She keeps it polished. If we hadn't looked closely to try to get to know Vivien, we would not have stumbled onto a couple of themes—faith and mother-hood, and we wonder how we might make these themes resonate—not to mention the fact of her hearing loss, which can result, if serious, in frustration, discouragement, anger, and isolation. We would not have known that appearances are quite significant to her. We wonder what we might do with that knowledge. Already we're writing about dementia, marriage, love, loss, and family, and we've barely started.

Now we've gotten to know these people better and we feel more confident. We proceed with our scene. Vivien says, "You dozed off." Jackie looks alarmed and says, "I've got to stop doing that." She says, "Do you know where you are?" "I'm right here." Vivien knows that waking is a dangerous time—anything could have happened while you slept. She'll change the subject. She says, "Your socks don't match." He says, "I have another pair just like them in the drawer." Well, he hasn't lost the ability to make a joke, she thinks. She tells him they'll be eating at seven or so and says he should freshen up and change into something more dressy. He stands and she tells him where the bathroom is. He says he knows where it is, but he walks to the fridge. Lately he's been losing everything, glasses, keys, books, sunscreen, shoes.

Vivien's on the computer chatting with her daughter Noelle, who still lives up in Massachusetts. Jackie's rubbing walnuts on the coffee table. Who knows why? He's piled the adult coloring books and the markers on the floor. Vivien tells her daughter that she should try to get here before the holidays are over. "This could be your father's last Christmas." Noelle types, "Geez, Ma, don't be so morbid. Anyway, we can't swing it this year. Besides, what's Christmas without snow?" Jackie stands up, admires the coffee table, and says, "Good as new." Vivien tells Noelle that her father has been forgetting to lock the doors at night and forgetting words in the middle of sentences. First it was names and then it was nouns. I do the bills now. I had to empty the junk drawer. Caught him trying to swallow a pencil sharpener. I found Nemo and Dory in his shirt pocket, poor babies. I had the garbage disposal unhooked. Afraid he'd stuff his hand down there. When Noelle tells her mother once again that she should get help, Vivien says, He's my husband and I can take care of him. When Noelle says, He won't get better, Vivien says, They're doing miraculous things with medicine these days. It's just a matter of time. Jackie's looking over her shoulder at the screen. He says, Who are you writing to now? She isn't worried he'll be alarmed—all he sees is gibberish. His reading days are over.

Whose story will we write? His or hers? One central character, remember. Our choice depends on the themes we'd like to explore, on the character who intrigues us more: the one with the most to lose, perhaps. We decide it's Vivien's story, and what she wants is to take care of her husband, and to care for him by herself, to make his decline as peaceful and comfortable as possible, and maybe even arrest the decline, to salvage, at the very least, what she can of their life and love together. Her desire to care for him must be considerable because the obstacles will mount, because motivation provokes action. And we think there can be no miracle, of course. Right now the obstacles are Jackie's behavior, the doctor's advice, and her daughter's indifference. Why does she do it? Because she loves him. And maybe that's sufficient reason alone to act. She owes him for all the years of security and love that he provided. She's grateful. To ship him off to a facility would make her feel guilty and ashamed. She knows what people would think. Every time she tries to care for Jackie, we'll write a scene. In fact, we might simply proceed by writing these obligatory scenes right up to the climactic moment.

But first we have to decide who's going to tell the story. Vivien can tell her story, or a third-person narrator can tell it and grant the reader access to Vivien's thoughts and feelings. And maybe to Jackie's—we'll see. All first-person narrators are unreliable to some degree because they have a stake in the outcome. Vivien would not like to be seen as heartless, for example. If we want Vivien's reliability to be a part of our story, we'll let her tell it. If we'd rather focus on her determined struggle to care for her husband, we'll choose a third-person narrator. So let's do that.

So now we have a central character, and we know what she wants and why she wants it. Now she has to struggle to get what she wants despite opposition. Conflict is at the heart of every story. So let's jump ahead a bit after Jackie returns to the room and Vivien orders Chinese takeout. Who has time to cook, what with trying to keep Jackie out of trouble? Jackie's admiring the coffee table. She repeats, You couldn't do what I asked? He says, What? You're dressed like a rodeo clown. He says, Can you ever stop criticizing me? She says, I wanted tonight to be special, that's all. Jackie shakes his head. She tells him she's ordered food. He says he's not hungry. She says, You're going to ruin another holiday? And the argument intensifies. Vivien thought she was making the evening special for Jackie, helping him to remember Christmases past and the love of family, and all she's done is drive him further into his disorder. She can't give up, of course.

The phone plays "Jingle Bells." It's Noelle. Vivien talks to the grandchildren. And then she tells little Arlo that Grampa can't wait to talk to him, hands the phone to Jackie, and goes to the buffet to make drinks. When she returns, she sees the phone turned off and says, That was quick. He says, Wrong number. The doorbell rings. The boy from Five Chinese Brothers arrives with the lotus prawns and Happy Family. (And if we think that selection is a little too heavy-handed, we'll change it in revision. Nothing is carved in stone, and we know the Mongolian beef is superb.) Vivien tips the boy generously, wishes him a merry Christmas. Jackie asks him to come in for a cup of cheer. Thanks, but no thanks. Busy night. The legend on the paper sleeve for the chopsticks reads, Happiness, Salary, Longevity, Pleasure.

Jackie gives up trying to eat with the chopsticks, grabs a fork. When Vivien dribbles soy sauce on her chin, he wipes it up. He's so sweet, she thinks, trying to be so helpful. He talks some nonsense about people he says they were close to when they were first married and living in Millbury. Tubba and Grace, Fats and Irene. She nods and smiles. He's making things up to fill his empty memory bank. What was it the doctor said this morning? Comprehensive dementia care is called for in this case. She was happy when Jackie said no. She squeezed Jackie's hand and said, We're in this together. We'll work this out, she told Dr. Luft.

After supper, they sit on the sofa. She puts some Christmas carols on Pandora. She asks him if he remembers going caroling with the kids. He says, We never did. She says, Try to remember, hon. When "O Holy Night" plays, Vivien lays her head on Jackie's shoulder and shuts her eyes and she's back at midnight Mass at St. Stephen's with Patsy, and they're singing his favorite carol, their arms entwined, and she's young again and all her brilliant life stretches out before her. She wants to weep. O night divine!

She presents Jackie with his gift, opens it for him. It's a photo he doesn't recognize of their Christmas forty-four years ago. She wants to remind him who he is and what he's relinquishing with his collapse into oblivion. And she's doing this for herself, too, driven by the absence of any love she can feel, dazed by his recent indifference. She needs him back. After all, who is Vivien without Jackie? He stares at it. He turns the photo over, stares at

Vivien, says something she can't make out. You know I can't hear you when you mumble. So he says it louder. What do you think you're doing, Viv? You know that's not me in the picture. She knows better than to answer. The carol didn't work, the photo didn't work. He's tired. She'll try again in the morning. They'll Skype the kids. He has good days and bad days. Don't we all?

She's too wound up to sleep, so she takes up her book. We've seen her attending to Jackie's needs, trying to help him remember who he is, seeing to his health care. And now some alone time to recharge her batteries. Jackie's quiet, probably sleeping. We figure the book will tell us something about Vivien and have something to say about our themes. Let's see if the reading will strengthen her resolve. If the book business goes nowhere, we'll cut it. Our job for now is to get off the straight and narrow and explore the world we're creating. She's on the La-Z-Boy with her feet up and the reading lamp behind her shoulder. The novel's called *A Ghost of a Chance*. She reads the back cover. "He's a man from her past; she's a woman of the present. Together they have no future!" Yes, they do, Vivien knows. And we think—yes, the book will comment on our characters. She kicks off her slippers, wets her finger, and turns the page. "The man with the eye patch stepped onto the elevator behind her." Vivien enjoys romance novels because she knows that in the end, the heroine—Jocelyn in this book—will get what she wants—the family mansion that is her rightful inheritance—and find true love as well—in this case, with Sebastian.

Vivien comes to the point in the novel where Jocelyn learns that Sebastian's ex-wife, Tophelia, has been committed to a very pastoral and posh asylum upstate and that dear, sweet, forgiving Sebastian, in order to provide for her inordinately expensive care, has reluctantly accepted an executive position with Solomon Howell and Associates without knowing that Solomon Howell is Jocelyn's second cousin once removed and the very man who would rob her of her legitimate legacy. This is the start of the fifty or so pages that Vivien thinks of as the inevitable dark days of the romance, the storm before the calm. She yawns, rubs her eyes, stretches, and sees him sitting there on the sofa. "Jackie, what on earth are you doing out of bed?"

He looks up from his crossword puzzle, and Vivien sees that it's not Jackie at all. She closes her eyes and massages her temples. When she opens her eyes, the man is still there, and he's smiling at her. He wants to know if she needs anything. Yes, she needs to know who he is and how did he get into her house. She wonders why she's not frightened. Well, because she must be dreaming, of course. She fell asleep reading. But then she recognizes those alarming blue eyes. She says, "Patsy, what are you doing here?" It makes perfect sense that she'd dream about Patsy— the Christmas memory and the novel about an old admirer returning. She looks at her book and sees the letters on the page, but can't read the words. See, it is a dream.

Has Vivien conjured Patsy to life in her dream? Let's stay in the room and find out. Patsy says, All the excitement's worn you out. She says, What excitement? He says, The kids. The grandkids, the whole crazy dinner with your cousins from the trailer park. She says, What do you know about Jackie's grandchildren anyway? He says, We've been over this and over this, Viv. He walks over to Vivien and kneels by the chair. Yes, you were engaged to Jackie Paradise. But Jackie was killed in Vietnam. You know this. And after he died, you came back to me, and I was over the moon.

What just happened?

All this time, we thought we were writing a conventional and realistic story of a marriage in its final days and about a devoted wife who is determined to tend to her husband despite his dementia, despite his erratic behavior and occasional rage, despite her lack of expertise, despite the urgings of others to get him in a nursing home, and we knew, of course, she would not be able to accomplish what is impossible, but now we learn that Vivien's reality may not be our reality. We write a first draft to discover our world, and we have just discovered something surprising—maybe alarming. Is Vivien delusional? Is her delusion temporary? Is it just for tonight? We try to reassure ourselves that she is dreaming, but that doesn't feel right. (In writing a story, trust your intuition.) Her actual husband has just stepped onstage, hasn't he? What are we to do? Well, what we don't want to do is dismiss too quickly this shift that seems to be undermining our story. Let's follow the accident and see where it leads us. If it leads to a cul-de-sac, we'll reject it.

Maybe Vivien says, I'm just going to wake up now and end this nonsense, and Patsy says, Come on, now, I'll put you to bed. When she says, Jackie's in bed sleeping, Patsy says, I'll show you he's not. She notices the crèche and says, It's Christmas! Patsy says, You do remember. The Cognex is working. You're getting better. He takes her hands and kisses them. She wonders if you can do that in a dream—feel the pressure of lips like that. We're still in Vivien's head. It's still her story, but the story is not the one she imagined she was living. She still struggles to save her husband, but the struggle is seen through the lens of her corrupted mind, and she's struggling to save a dead man. Her actual struggle is to save herself, it seems to us now, is to wrest some kind of meaning from this cognitive chaos that she is only peripherally aware of. One way to save herself was to wrest back the life she was robbed of, the dazzling life she should have been living with Jackie, not this predictable life with Patsy that ends with her unhinged and helpless. These struggles, the real and the imagined, the ongoing conflict, must be resolved. Vivien can fail, in her own mind, and admit that she can no longer care for Jackie, this stranger who attacked her when she tried to stop him from wandering off. She can succeed. Jackie gets better with the new meds. He enjoys their walks together. He doesn't try that funny business pretending to be someone he's not. Patsy, indeed.

Here's a possible resolution that also addresses Patsy's elliptical plot to care for Vivien at home. Patsy gets the plush tabby off the bookcase, the toy cat she got as a gift from Jackie Paradise before he was deployed, the cat she retrieved from the storage unit months ago, the cat she has named St. James. Who knows why? He leads Vivien to bed, removes her robe, and tucks her under the covers. She holds on to St. James. Patsy sits on the bed and asks her to remember the honeymoon she says they never took. Boston, he says. Hotel Essex. Room 312. What she remembers is a New York City vacation with Jackie. But when Patsy mentions the swan boats, Vivien can see the gleam of the bright sun on the silver water, the Canada geese paddling along in the boat's wake, the day lilies growing along the shore. She says, We walked along the Charles, didn't we? For hours, Patsy says. And he hugs her. Vivien sees that she has settled Jackie down. She tells him he's her best boy. She'll call him Patsy if that's what he wants.

Our draft's pretty rough, but we'll smooth it out in revision. Stories aren't written but rewritten, and we have to have something to revise—a complete first draft. To expect too much from the first draft is to misunderstand the writing process.

The plot led, we followed, and now we have our causal sequence of events, our essential beginning, middle, and end, and now we go back and add the connective tissue of exposition, flesh out our existing scenes, and write the others we've discovered on the way, like the visit to Dr. Luft, the crazy dinner with the family that Vivien can't remember. And what about the scar over Vivien's eye? The crucifix ring? And we should do something with Patsy's curious tattoo. But what? We'll figure it out as we write because our ass is still in the chair, and now we're so excited, we don't want to get up.

Let's do that again

Let's do that again. This time let's slow down even more and illustrate the ways that the plot we're following will lead us to considerations of characterization, theme, setting, tone, point of view, and so on. And we'll start with Chekhov's advice.

> *You could write a story about this ashtray, for example,*
> *and a man and a woman. But the man and the woman are*
> *always the two poles of your story. The North Pole and the*
> *South. Every story has these two poles—he and she.*
> —ANTON CHEKHOV

And with that quote in mind, we might also note what Eric Hoffer had to say. I like to think he was reading Chekhov when he wrote: "It is the pull of opposite poles that stretches souls. And only stretched souls make music."

A man, a woman, trouble. Leo and Zoë Grant have been married for fifteen years. One day, seemingly out of the blue, Leo tells Zoë he's leaving her. And we'll pause here for a moment before we get ahead of ourselves.

We know that everything of importance in a story, and Leo's declaration is certainly that, ought to happen in scene. The struggle, whoever's it is, needs to be dramatized, not explained or summarized. We'll get back to this idea of showing, not telling, shortly. But first, let's get our story moving.

> *Consider the technical language of the arts themselves.*
> *A plot first meant a physical site and building plan, then*
> *the stage director's plot or blocking plan, then the*
> *action of the story blocked out.*
> —EDWARD O. WILSON

Follow the accident, fear the fixed plan.

–John Fowles

I believe that the writer should tell a story. I believe in plot. I believe in creating characters and suspense.

—Ernest J. Gaines

The Grants

Leo tells Zoë the marriage is over

So Zoë and Leo are in their bedroom. He's sitting on the edge of their unmade bed staring at the floor, apparently lost in thought. (We've heard that phrase a thousand times: *lost in thought*. But now, maybe for the first time, it takes on significance, suggesting, as it does, a man carried away from the physical world and wandering in the world of ideas and images. We make a note.) She's standing in a pool of light spilling from the closet and staring at herself in the triple mirror on the dresser. There are four of her. She can see Leo behind her in one of the angled side mirrors. We understand that with the appearance of the mirror, we have stumbled onto themes that we can explore if we want to: *reflection*, as in *image* and in *thought*; *vanity*; and the *other self*. We also realize that Zoë is not seeing the actual Leo, but the virtual Leo, the husband laterally inverted and untouchable. She's not thinking this, of course; we are. And then we remember what Borges said. "It only takes two facing mirrors to make a labyrinth." And we ask ourselves if our central character's struggle will be a maze, a confusingly intricate course of events. We'll find out. Right now Zoë's still looking at herself in the mirror, and when she cocks her head and lifts her chin, we wonder what she's thinking. *When did I become my mother?* Or, *That new moisturizer's making me break out.*

Leo stands, adjusts his tie, clears his throat. He's wearing a white shirt and black slacks. He wipes the vamps of his brown shoes, one at a time, on the backs of his legs. We look at Zoë and see that she's wearing a large and loose light blue bathrobe and gray fleece slippers. Leo checks his watch, pockets his keys and wallet, and picks up his briefcase from his desk. He walks past Zoë without squeezing her hand or kissing her cheek, as he usually does. He hesitates at the door, his hand on the glass door-knob. Without turning around, he says, "Zoë, I'm leaving you."

What does Zoë do or say? We've got the trouble we were looking for, certainly. We watch Zoë, watch her closely, intently. Maybe we have to close our eyes to do so. It strikes us that imagining a scene and writing it are like watching a movie. We stare at the characters and wait for them to act, and they do.

And maybe the mention of movies makes us consider how movies and fiction differ in the manner of their storytelling. If our story were a movie, we would have presented the viewer with the images mentioned. He would have seen Zoë (she's that actress who played the detective in a recent crime thriller); he would have seen the bed (one just like it in the Wayfair catalogue) and the dresser and Leo, and the sweaters folded on the closet shelf. He would have sat there passively sucking it all in. But this is fiction, which means that the reader is in on the creation of the story. We furnish a detail, the reader furnishes the room, as it were. We said *dresser*, and he had to see it. Was it maple? French provincial? How many drawers? We mentioned the unmade bed, and the reader saw it and saw the brief-case. We didn't tell him the color of the floor or its construction. Carpet, tile, or wood? And we didn't describe the briefcase—the reader created it.

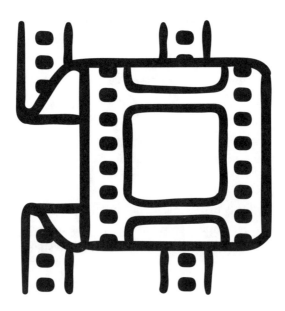

Plots are . . . what the writer sees with.

—Eudora Welty

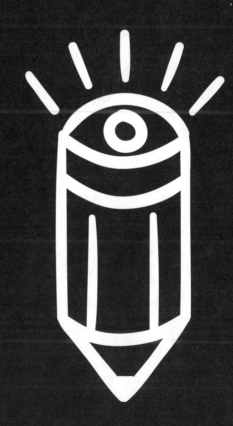

If you want attention, make a scene.

Scene & Summary

When you're writing a story there are two methods to use. We've said this before, and we'll say it again. You can show or you can tell. You'll do both. You'll write scene and you'll write summary. The differences between the methods:

Scene	Summary
+ Shows us	+ Tells us
+ We watch	+ We listen
+ Is dynamic	+ Is static
+ A close-up	+ A panorama
+ Simulates real time	+ Compresses time
+ We're an eyewitness	+ We're the jury
+ Is intimate	+ Is impersonal
+ We lean forward	+ We sit back
+ Reveals	+ Explains
+ Evokes	+ Invokes
+ Is about subtext	+ Is about text
+ Illustrates	+ Defines
+ We feel	+ We think
+ Is here and now	+ Is there and then
+ Is tense	+ Is composed
+ Is vivid	+ Is efficient
+ Is drama	+ Is explanation
+ Is particular	+ Is general

As we've said earlier in what is, of course, a generalization, overstated but reliable, everything important in your story should be shown in scene. Nothing unimportant should be shown in scene. No small talk.

Scene

An uninterrupted unit of dramatic action with a beginning, middle, and end, an unbroken flow of action from one incident in time to another. It makes no leaps in time or place, but it does allow for flashback or brief interruptions for background information or a character's mind drifting back in memory, for example. When you write a scene, you're saying this is important—so don't interrupt it or we'll think it could not have been all that important.

Scene brings action and dialogue to the reader, allows her to witness what is happening. A scene is psychologically in the present even if written in the past tense. Here's an example of summary and scene employed to present the same material.

Here's the exposition or summary:

"He opens the door and finds the place a mess, the body on the bed with a neat hole in the cheekbone."

Here's how the situation might be handled in scene:

"He opened the door, ran his hand along the wall, and found the switch. He saw her body on the bed, the message for him in lipstick on the mirror. The side of her face had been caved in with a blunt instrument. Blood leaked out of her ear. Her eye was opened. A hazel eye, the pupil dilated. He unwrapped the telephone cord from around her neck, followed it beneath the covers. He wiped the mucus and flap of skin off the telephone and called Reilly with the murder weapon. 'I found your niece, Teddy,' he said. He picked up a green matchbook on the night table from the Club Max in Boca. He noticed two spent matches in the ashtray. He said, 'Teddy, are you sitting down?'"

The temptation to explain should almost always be resisted. Feelings should never be told, but shown, for example. When you tell something you distance the reader somewhat, hold him away from the action. When you show, the reader looks on, participates, emotes. Knowing what scenes are required in a story is at the heart of the fictional art.

The opening

Leo is still standing there. Zoë has looked away from the mirror, but before she does anything else, we decide we need more information. Before we can draft the scene, we need to see the bedroom more clearly, and we need to learn more about this couple. We're going to know everything about that bedroom before we write the scene. And we'll come to know it by writing about it. Writing is how we see best. And we do so for the two reasons mentioned earlier. First, every detail in the room will tell us about the people who live there. Second, when people talk, they also do things, move, behave. (In conversation, for example, we are always talking with at least two languages, verbal and body, and they may not always be saying the same thing.) So we need to know the potential of the room. We need to know what our characters can do. So we see that the dresser takes up the wall between the closet and the bathroom, that there is a window by the bed with a covered radiator beneath it. Now that we're at the window, we can look out to see what Zoë can see. We can know the weather, the season, and perhaps something more about the place. So let's say it's early spring. The grass in the backyard is brown, the lilac bush has yet to blossom. There's a small pile of muddy snow by the cyclone fence. It's a sunless morning.

There's a water stain on the blue floral wallpaper above the dresser. The carpet is blue and buckled in places. The bathroom sink and tile are blue. We'll go into that bathroom soon, open the mirrored medicine cabinet to find out who's taking what and why. But first we'll note the items on the dresser: a faux-leather jewelry box with three drawers; a spray bottle of department store perfume; a box of tissues; a hairbrush and hand mirror; a bottle of cough syrup and a plastic spoon; a shallow bowl holding assorted coins, rings, and cuff links, and to our surprise, two framed photos of children in school uniforms—the Grants' kids. Jonah, eight, and Alicia, seven. They're upstairs sleeping. What this means is that the story just deepened and intensified. Leo is no longer leaving his wife; he's leaving his children as well, and he needs to take the responsibility for doing so. We won't let him forget it, and neither will Zoë. He needs to know that the children are going to think this divorce, should it come to that, is their own fault. They will be traumatized. We like the story better already. Zoë has tacked one of Alicia's first-grade drawings of the family to the wall by the mirror. The four of them are holding hands and smiling, And the sun above them is smiling. If we decide this is a bit too heavy-handed, we'll cut it—we can figure that out later.

Then we'll go through the dresser drawers, the mail piled on Leo's desk, see what bills they owe, what magazines they subscribe to (aspirations and enthusiasms), who's corresponding with them. We'll see what's on the walls. In fact, now we can see two framed vintage lithographs of perching birds, a cardinal and a finch. And over Leo's desk a calendar. Is it from a pharmacy? A church? A museum? Are there dates circled, doctors' appointments noted, music lessons? Let's say the calendar is from Blessed Sacrament Church. Writing a story is archaeology. And sociology. And detective work. We can never know too much about our characters. Revelations lurk in details, we know. We proceed with our opening scene. Well, not quite yet! Leo is still at the bedroom door and Zoë at the mirror. Did she hear what she thought she heard? We have a decision to make.

Our definition of plot implies several things. That there is *one central character*, not two. In the story of the difficult Grant breakup we must decide which of the characters is our central character. Whose story is it? His or hers? (We can write his story or her story, but not at the same time.) The emotional effect that we want the story to have on the reader will help us make that decision. As will other considerations, like: Which character are we more interested in? Which do we think the reader will find more interesting? Which is more compelling? What themes do we want to explore in the story? So, one central character per plot, and that central character must be active. Beginning fiction writers sometimes employ passive central characters, but we know better. No stories in which things just happen. Because things don't ever just happen. Divorce, for example doesn't just happen. It has a history. The character must want something; in other words, must be *motivated* to act and then must act.

We decide the story is Zoë's, will be told from her point of view. We're compelled by her situation and by the themes of loss, abandonment, and grief. We already know she must want to save the marriage or we'll have no story to tell. She can't say, What a relief; I was just thinking this marriage has run out of steam. Her motivation to save the marriage must be considerable and intense. We want to write about a woman out of options, a woman who will do whatever it takes to save her marriage. So: she doesn't think she can live without Leo; she believes that children need a father in the home; she was the child of divorced parents, and so she is acutely aware of the pain and the trauma involved and will not let that happen to her kids; she loves Leo. (And *love* alone would be enough motivation.) She will not let herself fail at the most important relationship in her life. Her whole life, her sense of who she is, her emotional and mental well-being are all at stake, as are her future and the futures of her children. Zoë knows that love abides, and damn it, she's not going to let anyone destroy her dream. She is going to do something, we can be sure.

We have our central character (Zoë), and we know what she wants (to save the marriage), and we know why she wants it (she loves him). And now she has to go after what she wants—despite opposition. The opposition is clear enough (Leo). Let's get back to that bedroom. Zoë knows that she didn't hear right. Leo turns. He repeats himself, this time looking into Zoë's eyes. But he doesn't let her respond. He starts right in on what sounds to us like a rehearsed speech, an apology, an argument. Leaving a marriage, we know, is not a spontaneous act. He points out the obvious—they hardly talk to each other anymore, make love infrequently and dispassionately. He says, "You're depressed half the time." She says, "I've got pills for that." (And we've discovered more trouble.) He says, "We don't have fun anymore," and she says, "A marriage isn't an amusement park." He tells her how this isn't easy for him. He doesn't want to hurt her. But he can't go on like this. Like what? Like just going through the motions. Zoë's incredulous. She says, "What the hell is going on?" He says, "I feel overwhelmed. I need some space right now." She might try to lighten things up and say, "Get a storage unit." Or maybe she explodes, but not before she closes the door so as not to wake the kids. She says, "You are not walking out on your family." He says, "I'm leaving." She says, "Over my dead body."

Leo's "needing space" remark is a cliché that we might want to reconsider, to rewrite, to get past the euphemism to the truth. Which brings up an important point. Our job in the story is not to blame Leo. What would be the point? No one person is to blame when a relationship runs aground. And as fiction writers we know that every person has his reasons. And our job is to understand them. Right now we don't like what Leo's doing to his wife, but at some point in the story he is going to get the opportunity to explain himself. Maybe every troubling character should get a shot at redemption. Not all of them will take it. Leo tells her he's rented a room for the time being. He won't be home tonight. He'll call at seven to talk with the kids. She says, What do I tell them in the meantime? She cries. She takes a tissue out of her robe pocket and blows her nose. She tells him she loves him. How could he do this to her? She says he owes her something after ten years of marriage. Leo touches his briefcase. She says, "This is killing me, Leo." We have now illustrated what Frank O'Connor called the three necessary elements in a story. Exposition: *Zoë Grant was a housewife in Worcester, Massachusetts*. Development: *One day her husband told her he was leaving her*. Drama: *"No, you're not," she said*.

We just discovered that the story is set in Worcester. And maybe this would be a good time to pause and to think about *place*. Every story has to take place somewhere. You can't move the earth if you have no place to set your lever. The setting colors the people and events in the story. Place connects characters to a collective and a personal past, and so place can be the emotional center of story. And by *place*, I don't simply mean *location*. A *location* is a dot on a map, a set of coordinates. *Place* is location with narrative, with memory and imagination, with history. A location becomes a place when we tell its stories. We are who we are because of where we grew up and when we grew up there. The home place shapes the way we think, and determines to some degree what we can and what we will think about. And every story is about the place where it unfolds as much as it's about the characters who live there and those who are just passing through. So take your characters and plant their feet on solid ground, and you'll be grounding the reader in your world at the same time.

*Every story would be another story . . . if it took up its characters
and plot and happened somewhere else. Imagine* Swann's Way *laid
in London, or* The Magic Mountain *in Spain . . .*
—EUDORA WELTY

Terroir is a word meaning the combination of factors including soil, climate, and sunlight that gives wine (or tea, or chili peppers, or maple syrup) its distinctive character. As with plants, so with people. Every city, town, neighborhood comes with a unique set of characteristics that identify the people who grow up there. And that's what we want. We want our characters to smack of the soil that nourished them.

*The . . . novel that fails is a novel in which there is no sense of place,
and in which feeling is, by that much, diminished. Its action occurs
in an abstracted setting that could be anywhere or nowhere. This
reduces its dimensions drastically and cuts down on those tensions
that keep fiction from being facile and slick.*
—FLANNERY O'CONNOR

There are also places within place. The story takes place in the character's community. The scenes take place in the homes, the businesses, the rooms, the offices, the parks and natural environments within that community. We visualize where our characters stand and sit and work and pray and play and walk and dream. We go there and apply our other senses. What can these places tell us about our characters? About their community? Think locally. We look at the world an inch at a time. One house, one condo, one apartment, one double-wide at a time.

For something to enter, a place must be made for it.

–J. G. Bennett

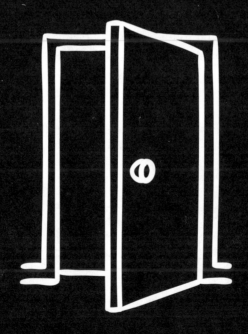

Writing about place

Time to write. If place is to be a character, it needs to do something, to act on your central character, and/or react to her. If place is character, you ought to be able to render its personality, its makeup, mettle, and mood, its attributes and temperament. So let's see how place affects both character and plot. Your central character goes for a walk. Seems innocent enough—until the place presents him with trouble. Write about all of this in your notebook. Try these three places:

Right now it's -22° in Arrowhead, Nebraska, at two in the morning. Your character has just left Basia's Lounge after an evening of Czech food and hard drinking, after last call and lights out. He, let's call him Ted for now, figures that he'll be fine after four hours of sleep. Ted's a trucker. He has to be in Omaha with his shipment by three in the afternoon. He's staying at the Relax Inn, and he thought it was a straight shot from the bar, but now he's not sure. The wind is howling and blowing the snow so that there's maybe three feet of visibility. And now he realizes he's forgotten his outer mittens at Basia's. His boots squeak on the snow. What if he's walking in the wrong direction? He can't feel his feet. He stumbles off a curb and falls. What happens next? And after that? Ultimately?

Al's Miata has broken down for the third and possibly last time on the Nevada 305 about halfway between Battle Mountain and Austin. Eighty-eight miles of nothing. Sand, rocks, and sage. It was a hundred and five when he left the service station in Battle Mountain with a new gas filter. No phone service. No water. No passersby. All he can do is walk and hope he gets picked up. He walks until his feet are swollen; he can hardly swallow, and he collapses on the side of the road. When he does hear a car approach and then another, he doesn't have the strength to get up. When night falls, he recovers enough to sit up and spots lights off in the distance toward the mountains and walks toward them. He comes to a small shack. He beats a vicious dog who attacks him. Hit him with a boulder, may have killed him. That'll be his secret. He knocks at the door—a shave and a haircut—the most nonthreatening knock he could think of. The door opens and a man with a rifle tells Al he has no water, no phone, no hospitality. Al says, I might die out there. Please. What happens next?

Now you get to write about a town you're making up. You just invented it. Give it a name and a location. As we did above. How is this place different from any other place? What are the local rituals that make it unique? Think about language, vocabulary, dialect, accent. Think about foods; think about the work people do. What are the annual events that everyone looks forward to? The schools, the architecture, the town or the neighborhood legends and characters. You're going to set a story here. Walk around the town or the neighborhood and put your five senses to work. Stop and talk to the people you find there—you're a writer in search of characters. Think about the seasons, the light, the ground, the schools, the churches. Walk down the main street and name all the businesses you see there. The public buildings. If there's a café, stop in. Look for the person inside who looks troubled. Sit next to that person and ask him what's wrong. He'll tell you. What does he say?

Back to our opening scene

Back to our definition a second: *one central character (Zoë) who wants something (to save her marriage) and goes after it despite opposition (as she is already doing)*. Conflict is at the heart of every story. *And as a result of a struggle* . . . It cannot be too easy for our central character to get what she wants. Zoë may tell Leo that he's being rash. She can beg him to stay: So we can talk. Please don't leave! The only thing Leo can't say is, Yes, you're right. That would be too easy. No struggle, no story. Zoë goes to Leo and throws her arms around him. He's not a monster. He feels terrible, but resolute. He's thought a lot about this. He says, We'll talk tonight. They hear the bare feet of their children hit the floor upstairs. Leo takes Zoë's arms from his shoulders. He apologizes. She can't speak. At the end of our opening scene, Leo walks out of the bedroom and out of the house.

It occurs to us that we've got another decision to make. Who is going to tell Zoë's story? Zoë can tell it, of course. A third-person narrator can tell it and grant us access to Zoë's thoughts and feelings. Those are essentially our choices. (Zoë can pretend to be talking about a character named Zoë, whom she calls *You*—she needs to distance herself from the pain, perhaps. *You're standing in front of the bedroom mirror, remembering your mother, checking the rash on your face, when your husband turns to you and casually announces that he's leaving you*. But this is first person in disguise. We could also have a third-person narrator who refused to grant us access to any character's thoughts or feelings, but why would we? Isn't the real drama below the surface?) This would be a good time to stop and think about point of view.

More fiction fails because the author has not had the discipline and ingenuity to provide and sustain a means of perception than for any other single reason.

–William Sloane

You never really understand a person until you consider things from his point of view.

–Harper Lee

Point of view

We write the story, but a narrator tells it. Our choice of narrator is a question of POV. Who is speaking and how? Through whose consciousness is the story understood? Point of view is how both the reader and the writer come to understand the story. Here is an opening of a story told in three different points of view:

First Person:
I'm thinking about the smoked salmon dinner with garlic mashed potatoes and grilled asparagus we'll enjoy when this hike is finally over.

Second Person:
The arch of your right foot aches and so does the muscle that runs down the outside of your calf.

Third Person:
He trips on the exposed root of a scrubby piñon pine.

More important than person (first, second, or third, as above) is distance—how close are we to the hearts and minds of the characters? And to what depth do we delve?

Choosing the right POV

Which POV will most effectively and efficiently address our goal and explore the values and motivations of the characters? Which POV will best answer the question, Why?

The answers to the following questions might also help us make our decision about an appropriate point-of-view character or characters:

+ Which character is the most troubled?

+ Which can be present at the obligatory scenes?

+ Which will change as a result of the struggle?

+ Which are you most interested in?

+ What do you want the reader's emotional and rational experiences to be?

We tell stories about ourselves in first person. So that may seem natural. But all fairy tales are in third. So that may seem authentic. Let's take a look at each of the points of view.

First person

The pronoun *I*. Or perhaps *we*.* There are three forms:

The informant I:
I'm in my apartment putting together a home entertainment center when the phone rings, and It's my ex's husband with the sad news that my son has died.

The reminiscent I:
It was ten years ago today. Snowing like crazy outside. I was in the den putting together an entertainment center when the phone rang, and my ex's husband told me that my boy had died.

The unreliable I:
I knew the call was coming before the phone rang because I'm cursed with knowing the future, and I knew what the call was about because I had dreamed of my boy in his coffin the night before.

As I said earlier, all first-person narrators are unreliable to some degree, since they have a stake in the outcome.

---

* My novel *Louisiana Power & Light* is written in first-person plural POV, a technique I took from William Faulkner's "A Rose for Emily." *LP&L* begins: "You're there, and here we are in Monroe, Louisiana, City of Steady Habits, Crossroads of Pipelines, Corrugated Paper Capital of the North Delta Parishes, elevation 65 feet, population, 56,600. And you, where you are, and we here, are all of us situated about halfway between stars and atoms . . ."

The pros of first person:

It's easy to get into and get to know the central character because you are always in his head.

It's immediate and has the authority of an eyewitness.

Every word tells us about the central character, the person speaking.*

It's easy to tell if you've violated POV.

The cons of first person:

That reliability problem: Is the narrator telling us the truth? Would he know the truth if it bit him in the butt? Unreliability can, of course, become a part of the story. The narrator may be unreliable through mendacity, naïveté, or insanity.

We're stuck with one mind and with one diction.

We see the narrator less clearly than we see others.

---

* Because we don't want a first-person narrator who is not the central character. Rust Hills points out in his book *Writing in General and the Short Story in Particular* when POV fails it is often because the POV character is not the character moved by the action.

Second person

The pronoun *you*. There are a couple of forms.

You is a **character** in the drama, making the viewpoint a lot like first person. There are a couple of ways second person works, which I'll call *"the reader as character"* (nice trick if you can pull it off) and *"the I-substitute."*

The reader as character:

That evening after supper, after you pruned the wisteria, walked the dog, set the recycling bins by the sidewalk, you go into the den and turn off the TV. You tell Emma you need to talk. She folds her paperback novel, looks at her watch, says, "My show goes on at nine." You lean over and kiss her on her forehead. "It's about work." You open the liquor cabinet, take out the sherry and two cordial glasses. You tell it just how you rehearsed it, how you wanted, needed, really, to change your life, how you'd been numbed by the routine of law practice and jaded by the legal system, disgusted by it, really. Here the reader is asked to imagine herself a character in the story. This can draw the reader into the story if we do it right, or put her off if we don't. This story deals in speculation, with what might be but is not, and since it's rooted in our common desire to start over, to get a second chance, to find redemption, to leave a miserable job, we hope the reader will enjoy the opportunity to pretend to be this man who is about to start over.

The I-substitute:

In your dream the two of you are walking in front of Old Main, and when you tell him about the trouble you're having with your narrative, he tells you you're doing it all wrong. "It doesn't breathe," he says. "Story! Story! Story! Goddammit," he says. "What do I do?" you say. He says, "Bring in a cousin from Illinois." He sucks on his True, exhales the smoke out the side of his mouth, and waves it away from his eyes. "Even better, have a man with a gun walk through the door. Something's bound to happen. Have him burst through the fucking door waving a .38 Ruger in front of his face. Let him fire a shot through the empty Morris chair." "You think?" you say. "And suddenly the story deepens like a coastal shelf," he says. This is a not very subtly disguised first-person point of view. It's the young writer we're hearing. He's distancing himself from himself and from the reader, moving his ego offstage.

Considerations with second person:

 Seems to work best in present tense and in shorter pieces.

Always experimental, so it can grab the reader's attention.

 The I-substitute can become annoying and distracting; it's a bit of a gimmick.

 The reader may not be able to see himself in the character, and the dream is broken.

 Addressing the reader, by the way, as I did in the *LP&L* example earlier, is not second person. It's a figure of speech called apostrophe.

Third person

The pronoun *he* or *she*. Several forms.

Third-person objective:

(aka dramatic point of view, camera lens, or fly-on-the-wall technique)

He's in a house in a Hopper painting, a house in Truro, a half mile through the moors to the beach. The windows are shuttered and blank. The house is silent. Those who live here are outside standing in the sun, their lengthening shadows still. No clutter in the closets, no pictures framed on walls. No cellar, no attic, no memories, no dreams. No dust in corners, just this studied violence of furniture arranged. Drawers, chests, cabinets, and wardrobes—some need for secrecy. The oak floorboards creak as he walks to the door and throws it open, letting the universe in. In this dramatic viewpoint, you must illustrate thought and emotion through speech, through imagery, through tone, and through behavior in the way that a screenwriter must (though you don't have the blessing of music to help you insinuate tone), the way that a playwright or actor must.

Third-person limited:

(aka third-person attached)

We get the thoughts and feelings of the central character and no one else. We can be both inside and outside the character as we are here:

Grady and Alice Bell's twenty-year-old daughter Hope has died. They're home alone after the funeral and the burial and after the distressing but obligatory reception for family and friends here at the house. Alice is slumped in a corner of the sofa, a sweater draped over her shoulders. She's blotting her swollen eyes with tissues and holding a porcelain teacup in her hand. Grady sits in a ladder-backed chair, elbows on his knees, staring at his left hand in which he grips a fistful of dirt he's taken from Hope's grave. He believes that if he had been listened to, Hope would still be alive. People are like dirt, he remembers his uncle Elwood saying. They can nourish you and help you grow or they can stunt your growth and hasten your death.

If one of the benefits of first-person narration is intimacy and immediacy, we get that as well in third-person limited. We're close to Grady here, but the narrator can also see Grady from the outside, can describe his appearance, for example, and is not restricted to just his consciousness. Can see what Grady does not. Alice on the sofa.

Multiple selective omniscience:

The viewpoint shifts from one character to another. We do it early in the story if we're going to do it at all. The trick is not to confuse the reader. The narrator can also pull out of the minds of the characters and into his own consciousness to give us another take on the characters' behaviors. Stephen Crane's "The Open Boat" shifts points of view: *"The cook squatted in the bottom and looked with both eyes at the six inches of gunwale . . . The correspondent, pulling with the other oar, watched the waves and wondered why he was there."*

Third-person omniscience:

The narrator as god. The almighty voice of the epic. Can know anything about any character, can be in any place at any time, past, present, future. A problem with the omniscient narrator is focus. He can tell all, but he shouldn't. He may tend to wander and to digress, and our job is to rein him in, appear to digress, but don't. And as with a first-person narrator, he has a tendency to tell and not to show. He's an authority, and so he assumes our trust. We'll believe what he says. He forgets that scenes do more than earn our trust. Scenes engage our emotions. Anna Karenina begins: "Happy families are all alike; every unhappy family is unhappy in its own way."

Interior monologue and **stream of consciousness** are usually associated with third-person points of view.

Interior monologue:

We aren't told what the character thinks, so much as we experience the thought itself. We are in the mind of the character. There is *direct interior monologue* and *indirect interior monologue*. The passages quoted below are from *Deep in the Shade of Paradise*. Our lawyer Rance is in the middle of questioning his own client on the stand.

Direct:

"Rance wondered why in blazes he took this case anyway. Why was he a lawyer at all? He never wanted to be a lawyer. He'd just have to tell his wife tonight that's all. Emma, he'll say, honey, I have to quit. I'll call Jack on Sunday, meet him out at the club. We'll talk. I'll tell him my heart's not in it anymore. I'll stay on till he finds someone else." No intermediary processed the thoughts for us. Rance's actual thought is rendered. He really did think, "Honey, I'll have to quit."

Indirect:

"He'd like to be with her now instead of in the courtroom. He'd draw the living room curtain, put on a Mozart's Violin Sonata in C, *Andante Sostenudo*, pour two glasses of Pedro Ximénez sherry, touch her knee. She might ask him, What will you do now, dear?" Rance did not really think, "*He'll* draw the blinds." He thought, "*I'll* draw the blinds." This allows the narrator to be both inside and outside the character.

Free indirect style:

Another term for this technique, a way of narrating characters' thoughts or utterances that combines some of the features of third-person report with some features of first-person direct speech, allowing a flexible and sometimes ironic overlapping of internal and external perspectives. Free indirect style dispenses with tag-phrases ("she thought," etc.), and adopts the idiom of the character's own thoughts, including indicators of time and place, as in, "She'd leave Dodge tomorrow," rather than "She decided to leave Dodge the next day." Free indirect style may dispense with quotation marks, transpose the present tense of direct speech into past tense, and change first person into third person.

The Plot

Stream of consciousness:

A term coined by Henry James's brother William. Stream of consciousness tries to record the flow of the countless incessant, meandering associations and impressions that impinge on the consciousness and rational thoughts of a character. Unlike direct interior monologue, which it resembles, stream of consciousness is not as solicitous of the reader and does not try to edit, arrange, or clarify the thoughts. The following from *Ulysses*: "He walked on. Where is my hat, by the way? Must have put it back on the peg. Or hanging up on the floor. Funny, I don't remember that. Hallstand too full. Four umbrellas, her raincloak. Picking up the letters. Drago's shopbell ringing. Queer I was just thinking that moment. Brown brilliantined hair over his collar."

When I hear the word "stream" uttered with such a revolting primness, what I think of is urine and not the contemporary novel.

–James Joyce

It doubles your perception, to write from the point of view of someone you're not.

–Michael Ondaatje

Writing different points of view

1. Imagine that a marriage of long standing has just ended. Why? What happened? How did love turn to . . . what, indifference? Surely not hate. Let her tell the story of the breakup and the divorce. And then let him. Now let's say they have a child. Let the child tell his version of the endgame.

2. I've heard students claim that a man can never and should never write from the point of view of a woman. (And vice versa, of course.) I mention Emma Bovary and Molly Bloom. I've heard students say that a white American has no right to set a story in Haiti or France, for that matter. We ought only write about our own culture, and that culture ought to be defined as narrowly as possible. These are students who seem tragically lacking in imagination. They seem unable, unwilling, and uninterested in empathizing with others. Our job as storytellers, however, our privilege as fiction writers, is to imagine and inhabit the lives of others. We remain sensitive to differences and don't write about what we don't know about. So let's try it now. Write a two-page or longer monologue by a character of the opposite gender. Last night he or she learned some terrible news. What was it? Let the character tell you.

3. Three people observe the identical landscape. Let's say they're on a wooded hill, and they're looking down on a meadow, a brook, a farmhouse, a barn, and a forest beyond. Let each of them describe what they see, hear, smell. The first person is dying, but don't tell us he or she is dying. The second person is pregnant, but don't tell us that. The third person is a visual artist.

Our story

We left Zoë alone in her bedroom. She had tried to convince Leo to stay and talk, but failed. She cannot give up, of course. This is a struggle, and that means that the action will be protracted. Every time she tries to save the marriage, we'll need a scene. So what are the scenes we'll be obliged to write at the very least? Well, for now, let's leap ahead to sometime that afternoon when Zoë arranges for her friend Betty Ann to pick the kids up after school, screws up her courage, and drives herself to Leo's workplace. We saw him in that shirt and tie, saw the briefcase. What does he do? It's Worcester, a medical center, so maybe Leo's a doctor at UMass Memorial, but something about that buckled carpet and stained wallpaper suggests not. So let's have Leo be an admired high school guidance counselor. He's overworked and underpaid.

Zoë confronts Leo at work

Zoë walks right past the front office without getting a visitor's pass and into the teachers' lounge. She sees Leo at the end of the table drinking a can of soda and eating a vending machine snack. She says, "We need to talk," and when she does, the three other teachers in the room go quiet and cast their eyes to the table. Leo says, "Let's go to my office." As in our first scene, we'll need to know what the setting—in this case Leo's office—looks like. We need to know if that family photo is still on his desk. We need to know the source of light. Zoë tries to reason with Leo. She wants to know where he's staying, what he's planning. Is he coming back or what? She says they ought to go to marriage counseling. He owes her at least that much. Leo says this is neither the time nor the place. She says, What's more important to you than your marriage and your family? Zoë had come to the office with hopes of convincing Leo to come back home where he belongs, but her pain is overwhelming her and distancing Leo. She can see this is going nowhere. It's only making matters worse. Once again, the only thing that Leo can't say is, All right I'll be home tonight. He does say he's found a place to stay and won't be coming home just yet. Zoë can't breathe. She tells Leo that she's not going to say anything to the kids. He's the one that's going to tell his children, who adore him, that he's leaving them.

And now we see that we've discovered another scene to write. And we realize that this might be the scene where Leo explains himself to his kids, speaks honestly, earns our esteem. We don't know why he left, do we? He hasn't told Zoë why. Of course, by the end of the story, he will. If we must, we'll lock him and Zoë in a room, and we won't let them out until they've been honest, until they've pushed past the clichés ("midlife crisis," "love but not in-love," "you've changed") and gotten down to the fears and the dreams and the anger, and whatever else is down there. Sometimes characters don't want to deal with their emotional issues. And sometimes we find ourselves as writers happily abetting their avoidance. We do that because this is the hard part and because we don't want to have to deal with our own emotional issues, either. But we must. If the character is reticent or evasive, try locking yourself and the character in a "room," and sit there talking until you both get down to the truth, as in the interview that follows my little foray into cognitive behavioral therapy.

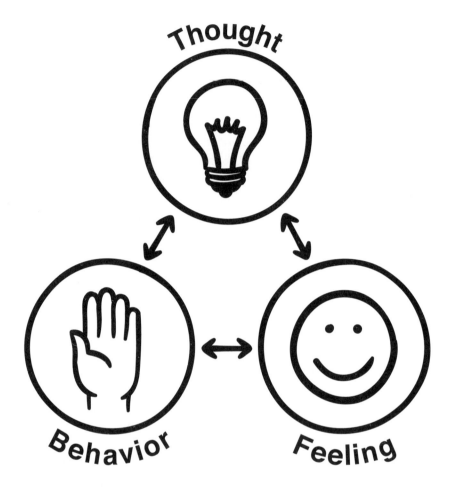

Cognitive behavioral therapy tells us that our thoughts, feelings, and behaviors are interrelated. We think our spouse is ignoring us, and that makes us angry, and we give him the cold shoulder, a taste of his own medicine. The thought, we realize, may be erroneous. If you change any one of these three elements, the others will change. The easiest to change is behavior. If your character is behaving badly and you don't know why, you can become a therapist and question him about his behavior and listen to and write down his answers. And perhaps both of you will learn why he's doing what he's doing. And it's more important that you, the writer, know than he, the character.

Storyville!

Start doing something you like, and you'll feel better, and your thoughts will become more positive. This is a way we can think about your character as well. He's behaving nastily toward his wife, let's say. Why? Because he thinks she doesn't love him? Because he thinks she's holding him back? These thoughts make him resentful, etc. We're not in therapy, and we don't necessarily need him to change (unless he's our central character), but connecting the action to a thought to a feeling helps us to understand a character's motivation. If we want to, we can use the other characters to explore the husband's behavior. Why are you treating your wife like that? She doesn't love me. Why do you think she doesn't love you? And so on. Or we can be the counselor with our character off the page, as in the interview suggested on the following pages.

The Interview:
Peeling the onion

> You say your wife doesn't love you. Do you want to go with that?

>> I'd rather not talk about it.

> Well, you don't have a choice. This isn't really therapy. This is a story. We don't have time for lies.

>> I'm not lying.

> Our biggest lie is the one we tell ourselves. You believe what you've been telling yourself. You're not interested in the truth.

>> Well, she doesn't talk to me. She's not romantic like she was.

> Do you talk to her?

>> I try.

> Do you tell her you wish she was more romantic? Do you tell her you just want to talk? Do you turn off the TV when you tell her?

>> She knows.

If she doesn't love you, why are you with her?

We're married.

And . . .

That's it.

What do you want to happen?

I don't know.

Now we're getting somewhere.

What?

You didn't say you wanted the marriage to work out.

No, I didn't.

Why?

I'd rather not talk about it.

No need to blame. Just deal with the fact. You're not in love.

I suppose I thought it would be easier to live with myself if I thought she didn't love me.

Okay, we're past the cliché. Now let's see what's really going on. Tell me your story.

Back to our story

Leo thinks it through

Let's assume we just did a "therapeutic" interview with Leo and found out that he's in a lot of pain himself. This is the most difficult and most confusing thing he has ever done. And the cruelest. He had thought he was incapable of such ruthless behavior. We found this out because we asked a question, and then we shut up and let him talk. We wrote down what he said. He's baffled. He can't imagine not being with his kids. He can't believe that he would hurt someone whom he thinks he still loves, but may no longer feel passionate about. He's frightened and unhappy, and so is Zoë. He can see it. They've become dull, habitual, uninteresting. He has to do something. He doesn't want to wake up at sixty and find out he's wasted his life. Maybe that's too strong. Doesn't want to go through the motions. That's better. It's not Zoë he feels shackled to, but the marriage.

And now that he's taken the first step, he knows he can't go back. How much crueler would it be to go home now, only to leave again in a month or a year, to put Zoë through this hell again? Or worse, to stay with her but live his real life elsewhere? He doesn't want to drown in resentment. When he looks ahead to the best possible ending, he sees himself and Zoë, best pals, sharing a drink, talking about their marvelous and successful and entirely well-adjusted kids. He's starting to drift into a fantasy world. We take what he tells us at face value. Not everything rings completely true maybe, but we'll have plenty of time to chat with Leo again. All of this note-taking has let us into Leo's thoughts and feelings. But we've decided to tell the story from Zoë's point of view, so in the story we're not going to get internal access to Leo's thoughts and feelings. He'll have to articulate them in speech or in actions. (Unless we change our mind about POV.)

The world intrudes

We're thinking ahead to the scene with Leo and the kids, and so is Zoë. He's coming over Friday night after work. Meanwhile, the world intrudes on Zoë.

The kids need rides to school and to practices and appointments.

 Her mother's been calling about Easter plans—are they coming to visit or not?

 The kids want to know when Daddy's coming home; they miss him.

Betty Ann keeps asking if everything's okay. Zoë pretends it is. She's hoping that she can convince Leo to come home and that no one will ever know that there was a problem.

Zoë considers how many people would be affected by this divorce:

 Her family—it'll kill her father

Leo's family

 Their friends—they'll have to divvy them up like books and CDs

The kids

 The folks at the literacy program

Everyone at the PTA

 The kids at the dance school

The Little Leaguers

What will Father O'Brien think? She's trying to pretend that everything's okay, but she breaks down crying at the supermarket, at red lights. She can't listen to music, can't drive. She almost hit a child on a bike. She can't eat. The kids keep saying what's wrong, and she tells them she has a bad headache. She despairs, but then remembers Friday night when she'll have another chance to talk to Leo. They've been told he's away at a convention. He must be missing the kids. He must be tired of living in some cramped motel room. Zoë does not allow herself to think that the place he's found might be more spacious, might belong to another woman, that Leo might be finding all the solace and love he needs. She is so hopeful she can't sleep. She texts him with an invitation to supper on Friday evening. He texts that he'll be there at six.

We're making things difficult for Zoë because that's our job. We love her, care about her, but we're being as cold-blooded as we can be. And this is why: The harder she tries to get what she wants, the deeper she digs into her emotional resources the better we'll know her, and the better we know her, the better we'll like her, understand her, and care about her. We want to make it difficult for Zoë, but we don't want to beat her up. We want the obstacles to relate to her struggle to save the marriage. We could have given Jonah autism, for example. Could have had the car die in the middle of a traffic jam. Zoë herself might have learned she has breast cancer. The mortgage payments could be months overdue. And we may decide that one of those things could happen. But we need to ask if it will serve the plot and not diffuse the thematic issues in the story. We realize that we've focused on Leo as the single obstacle so far. We understand there may be others.

What about her own pain and humiliation? Is Zoë having to struggle past her own resistance to a reunion with Leo?

What if she confessed to Betty Ann over drinks, and Betty Ann says, We all wondered when you'd leave the son of a bitch. Zoë doesn't understand. She's not leaving; he is. What did her friends see that she has been blind to?

And so on. We jot some notes. We'll begin to fill in the narrative in the next draft. But for now, we leap ahead to Friday night.

The family supper

Maybe Zoë has had her hair done. She's dressed the kids in their best clothes. She's prepared Leo's favorite meal. Is it bone-in ribeye, mashed potatoes, and asparagus? Or does that make Leo too ordinary? (Already we're thinking of the reversal at the imminent supper table; can't wait to write it. But first—the favorite meal.) Zoë prepares maple roasted chicken quarters, a side of green peas with crispy bacon, and a side of mac and cheese. She checks the kitchen clock. Time for us to explore that kitchen. Zoë's standing over the gas stove. A microwave is on the counter beside her. There's a set of aqua chalkboard canisters between the microwave and the Keurig coffeemaker. The sink is a double basin and is stainless steel. Above the sink is a window, and on the sill, an African violet. We're going to look in the refrigerator to find out what the Grants are eating. We'll open the freezer and the vegetable drawers. We'll know who's on a diet and who has a sweet tooth. We'll go through the junk drawer.

Leo rings the doorbell, which rattles Zoë. (He has just announced that he no longer lives or belongs here!) The kids go crazy. Leo gives them the new toys he's bought. A watercolor paint set for Alicia and Legos for Jonah. Zoë makes him a martini. He sits with the kids on his lap in his favorite chair. He looks around the room like he's never been here. And we look with him. We're in the den. The photo of Leo and Zoë on their honeymoon in Provincetown is still on the TV. The magazines on the coffee table seem to be arranged more neatly than usual. The kids want to know what they're doing this weekend. Slow down, Leo says, one at a time. We remember that definition of plot as motivations in collision. Zoë's plan: save the marriage. Leo's plan: eat and run.

They all sit down to supper in the dining room. A while ago Zoë got on a Rural Americana kick and bought this reclaimed wood trestle farm table and four metal cross-back dining chairs. She bought a hutch to match, a dry sink, and two faux-primitive paintings of children playing with barrel hoops. What do these details reveal about Zoë? Leo picks the bacon out of his greens and pushes the mac and cheese to the side of his plate. Jonah says, Daddy, eat everything on your plate. Leo tells him, Daddy's on a diet, and immediately knows he shouldn't have said that. And so do we. And so does Zoë. She feels like she's been hit in the face with a shovel. The son of a bitch has a girlfriend. Zoë stands and hurries out of the room. She has a good cry in the bathroom. She can hear Alicia telling Leo that Mommy cries all the time. Zoë doesn't want her tears to frighten him, doesn't want him running from her obvious pain. She pulls herself together. When the kids go to bed, they'll talk. And who knows, he may stare into the faces of his kids and realize what a fool he's been.

After the disastrous dinner

Later, back in the den, we see how hurt Leo really is, how wonderful and loving and honest he is with the kids. He tells them how he and Mommy need to spend some time apart. Zoë can't help it—she interrupts: Daddy needs to spend time apart. Leo does what he can. He hugs the kids, kisses them, tells them he'll call them every night and see them whenever they need him, whenever they want him. He's doing what he can. Zoë is beside herself. How can he go through with this? The kids are screaming. They want to go to Daddy's house. That wouldn't be a good idea, he says. Zoë says, Daddy has a roommate, and regrets it immediately. Leo tucks the kids into bed, reads them stories, comes downstairs when they're asleep, says good night. Zoë wants to know about the other woman. Leo doesn't try to deny it. Zoë says, What's going to happen to me? Leo says he wishes he could see the future. Dismissive and cruel, we think. Is that what we also want the reader to think?

Even later, after several glasses of wine, Zoë texts a rambling message to Leo. She tells him he's killing her. Tells him he's destroying the children's lives. Tells him no one will ever love him the way she does. Don't expect your bimbo to hang around for very long, she texts. Jezebels never do.

If we were allowing ourselves a chance to shift points of view, we might write a scene here where Leo and his girlfriend, call her Layla, read the message. Layla is so understanding, feels so appropriately guilty. She knows the pain that Zoë must feel. She knows how this is tearing up Leo. They didn't want this, didn't want to fall in love. It just happened. She never dated married men, but it was different with Leo. And then we might stick around and listen to Leo be more honest with Layla than he has been with Zoë or with himself. And maybe we learn that he doesn't want to live without passion in his life, and he has for too long. And so on. Now, if we think all this information is so intriguing and important that we need it in the story, then we'll rethink our point-of-view decision.

One month later

Leo shows no signs of coming home. The first night the kids went to their dad's for a sleepover, Zoë was miserable. She couldn't stand the silence in the house. She turned on televisions in several rooms for company. But she's not alone, and she finds that out when she tells her friends and family, at last, what's going on. She gets nothing but love and understanding and attention. Betty Ann tells Zoë, Whatever you decide, I'll be there for you. Zoë says, I *have* decided—I want Leo and my family back, but I have no control over that. Zoë's dad—let's call him Oliver—says she and the kids never have to worry about a thing, not money, not a place to live, not anything, as long as he and Mother are around.

What we're exploring is Zoë's world, and we're learning things about her we didn't know earlier, and we see that folks are making it easier for her to move on. And she'll have to struggle against that as well, won't she? What about her own pain and humiliation? Is Zoë having to struggle past her own resistance to a reunion with Leo? We jot some notes. We'll begin to fill in the narrative in the next draft.

A couple of events embolden Zoë

Let's say on the next weekend that the kids are due to go to Leo's, Jonah and Alicia tell her they don't want to go. They don't have fun over there. Dad talks more to Layla than to them. She feels both relieved to have them home with her and angry that her children are not a priority in their dad's life. So she calls him up to tell him what the children have said, and he is duly apologetic, and the conversation turns toward the future, as it must. His evasive answers are infuriating, and Zoë tells him he has to make a decision one way or the other, and he says he knows that. What kind of answer is that? she says. And suddenly she realizes he's not confused at all. His not deciding what he wants *is* a decision. He's not going to counseling; he's not going to ask for a divorce; he's not ever going to bring up the subject of their marriage. And so he's forcing her to make the decision, to say, I can't take it anymore. She asks him to meet for dinner. He agrees. We need to talk—about the kids, about us. They agree to meet at the Brasserie, their favorite restaurant. Maybe this is where Leo proposed to Zoë.

Let's go back to our earlier definition of plot for a moment. Motivations in collision. We need to think about what Leo and Zoë want from this dinner date. Zoë is still trying to save the marriage, but she needs Leo to decide and decide right now. Decide to come home, to try counseling— and to do so he needs to leave his little sweetie, decide something. Have the goddam courage to do something. Think about other people for once in your life. It's a risk she's willing to take.

Leo, on the other hand, is more convinced than ever the marriage is over. He believes in new beginnings. He realizes he can still be what he always wanted to be. He can change everything. He can be in a dizzyingly romantic relationship and still be a fabulous dad. He can take control, begin to live an adventurous life. And as a happier man, he'll be a better father, a more creative and productive counselor, an ardent lover. He'll be fulfilled. He doesn't know how he'll say this. He's glad that Zoë suggested the restaurant. There wouldn't be a scene in a public place. (Of course, we already know he's wrong about that.) And we realize we'll have the great opportunity to design a restaurant and come up with a menu. Maybe we'll base it on our own favorite restaurant. If so, we'll head there with our notebook and our smartphone camera, and we'll get the details we need. We'll photograph the menu. We'll jot down details of sound, smell, taste, and texture.

At the restaurant

Zoë is there first. She's on the cell to the kids when Leo joins her. He kisses her on the cheek. She hands him the phone. He talks to the kids, tells them to have fun at Betty Ann's, says he loves them. They order drinks and food. The conversation is cordial and cautious. Zoë is trying to assess Leo's mood and intentions, and she is, she realizes, giving him the opportunity to broach the unavoidable subject. She is disappointed, but not surprised, that he doesn't. He could go on with this small talk all night.

Zoë tells him she needs him. She says no matter what he decides, she'll always be there for him. She had one great love in her life and he is it. There won't be another. But you have to decide what you want. I can't wait around while you equivocate in your honey's arms. She knows that the longer he's with Layla, the harder it'll be to get him back. He falls back on his "I'm confused" excuse. He tells her he's started therapy to help him work out his issues. Zoë says she's happy for him, and even she's not sure of the tone of her voice, but she's not waiting for his eventual therapeutic epiphany. He needs to decide tonight. No, she's not kidding.

The waiter brings the dinners (blackened swordfish for him, grilled Atlantic salmon for her) and this gives us a moment to consider what's going through Zoë's head. She's waiting for an answer, but she has more to say. She wants to say she feels humiliated by him. He's made her feel unlovable and unattractive. But if she says all that, he'll only get defensive and withdrawn. She wonders if she should tell him that she parked outside his love nest one Saturday night, staring at the apartment windows. Should she admit that she was the vandal who hammered in the driver's-side window of Layla's Scion?

We hear utensils scrape the china plates. We hear Leo's jaw cracking as he chews. We note he's chewing more methodically than he usually does. We're paying attention, jotting the details down in our notebook. We can hear, and Zoë can, too, bits of conversation from other tables, the piped-in classical music, one diner's hearty laughter. We've just discovered how to write silence—describe unobtrusive noises. Zoë says, I'm waiting for your answer. Surely you've had time to think about this. Surely you've thought of nothing else. He says, It's not as simple as you're making it out to be. This is an important decision. She says, You bet it is. Tell me, Leo, are you coming home or not?

Leo says, You sound angry. I understand why you're angry. Maybe if we explored your anger— Zoë interrupts. Don't talk to me like I'm one of your troubled students! Heads turn at nearby tables. Leo says he won't stay here if she's going to act irrationally. Zoë says, Then tell me what you want from me. We look at Leo. He puts down his knife and fork. He takes a deep breath. He says, All right, you want honest, I'll give you honest. He speaks calmly. He tells her he's not coming back. She cries. He says, You know, you always want to talk, but if you don't hear what you want to hear, you cry, and that effectively ends the conversation. Do you want to hear this or not? She calls him a bastard. (Another reversal, we note: this is not what she had planned.) She accuses him of not ever loving her. He says he always thought he loved her, but now that he has experienced real love, he sees he did not. And we think he has gone too far and wonder if he is worthy of redemption and reconciliation. We'll tone it down perhaps in revision. Or not. Maybe the scene escalates further. Zoë's tears enrage Leo. Once he gets going he can't stop himself. He doesn't even care who overhears him. He tells her to get a lawyer. She tells him she'll take him for every penny he's worth. Says she'll get the house, get everything. He says she can have everything. She says he'll never see his kids. He says, No court would agree to that. Let's talk sense, he says. It's over, where do we go from here?

Maybe that happens or maybe they both are too afraid to push the issue any further. They mollify each other for the time being. Zoë because she needs the hope to go on living, Leo because he needs to think he's being as considerate and caring as he can be, given the hideous circumstances. We'll find out when we write the scene. At any rate this brings us back to the definition: let's see, a central character who wants something, goes after it despite opposition, and as a result of a struggle, comes to a win or a loss. There must be a resolution. The central character gets or does not get what she wants. Leo runs off with Layla. (We make a note to get to know Layla better than we do. She's not central, but she's integral. We don't even know how old she is. [Every story is many stories.]) Or he agrees to go to marriage counseling to try to work things out. He's not promising anything. He's had to break up with Layla when he missed his kids so terribly and saw their pain. He'd try to make it work for their sake. Maybe he thinks it won't work, but he'll play the dutiful husband with the mistress across town. And then he remembers how he dreaded turning into that person.

Remember that we don't need the resolution of Zoë's life, just the resolution of the problem. As a result of this action, the plot, the central character is changed. The change in the central character can be dramatic. Zoë is alone, but realizes that she has the strength to go on. Or she gets Leo to agree to come back. We're all hopeful the marriage will be saved. Or the change can be more subtle, like the revelations James Joyce called epiphanies. Zoë sees Leo with Layla, and what she sees convinces her that she has never given him the love that this woman displays. However we resolve the story, we'll resolve it in scene. So let's do that now. Zoë and Leo are back together. We need to think scene again to close the story. She's gotten what she has struggled so courageously for. We admire her so. We like symmetry, and so we decide to close the story where we started it.

And in the end . . .

Zoë is at the mirror, brushing her hair. She's cut it short, colored it sable. Leo 's in bed with his iPad, as he reads something by Wayne Dyer called *Manifest Your Destiny*, and it's full of all that Joseph Campbell kind of crap like "Follow your bliss," something only a man could say and only a man could get away with. He has a cup of coffee on the bedside table. He slurps as he drinks. Zoë watches him move his lips as he reads whatever he's reading. She's beginning to realize that getting Leo back is not the victory she had expected. In fact, it's a prison sentence, isn't it? She's married, yes, but she has been so humiliated and hurt by him that she knows the relationship can never be the same again and that she will never stop resenting him for the pain. She knows that she's the loving one, that she's the strong one (she's had the strength to be weak), and yet she's the one who suffered and who has been made to feel guilty and inadequate.

We're not done quite yet. We do have a simultaneous reversal and recognition. But how do we end? Not with her thoughts. Too static, too literal. What we'd like to happen to the reader is that when she closes the book, the final image stays with her, and she can't get that haunting picture, that freeze-frame, out of her head. What is different about that bedroom from when we first saw it? A difference that might indicate an emotional change? Is the answer out the window? Have the lilac blossoms faded? Is it something about the mirror? Is it cracked? We're not sure yet, but we're confident now that after another draft or two or three, after looking more closely, after spending more time with these two, after getting to know them better, we'll find just the image we need. And probably we'll be watching Zoë do something in that final sentence of the story that so moves us, that is so surprising, and is so right, that we are stunned. We didn't know we could write this well. And we put the story aside and enjoy the moment, walk around town like we own it, knowing that in the morning we'll have the great pleasure of getting back at the story once again.

Exercise 1:

The Stranger

Here's a familiar plot device: A stranger rides into town. You've been that stranger many times in your life. At the new job, in the new neighborhood, at you first college party. Perhaps you changed schools and got dropped into this sixth-grade class of longtime friends, and you were scared to death. You saw the other kids staring at you, whispering and laughing. Then the teacher said, Tell us all about yourself. You've also watched strangers ride into your life. Like the day you looked up from your desk at the clinic to see a man walking toward you, and you sensed trouble in his resolute stride and his icy demeanor. He told you he knew about your affair with his wife. She was an old flame, it turned out, someone you hadn't seen in years. No, he said, it's not a joke. Why would she do this to you? To him? Let's take this outside, he said. What did you do? Take a look back at the times in your life when you felt assaulted by a stranger or felt that you did not belong and were not welcomed. That's the kind of trouble that we develop into stories.

Exercise 2:

The Quest

Here is another familiar plotline: A person sets off on a quest. What in your life have you started out to find? Why that? Did you find it? How? Why? Why not? What were the obstacles in your way? Have you given up? What are you seeking now? Where are you looking? Write a narrative about a literal or figurative journey that you've taken in search of beauty, bliss, enlightenment, friendship. What has been your most important journey? Crossing a room can be as perilous as crossing the Atlantic. Think of the time you went to your boyfriend's mother's wake to comfort your boyfriend, you thought, and you caught a ride home with his friend, and you didn't know it then but you had discovered your future husband.

Exercise 3:

Taken by Surprise

List as many ordinary activities as you can in five minutes. Eating in a restaurant, writing a letter, washing the dishes, watching TV, etc. When the list is finished, go back and include a specific character performing each activity. A teenage boy washing the supper dishes, a nun writing a letter, and so on. This will be your opening sentence. Now add a sentence of complication. The nun's letter is a resignation after twenty years in the convent. The teenage boy sees the lights of his father's car enter the driveway. Ask the questions suggested by the situation. Answer and begin. Start with the reporter's questions (how? what? where? why? when?) and then ask more specific questions based on the answers given. Try the following and write as many of your own as you can: 1. A bank teller gets off the bus at Third Street as she's been doing for the past six years. The bank building, her place of employment, is being demolished. 2. The vice principal reads the morning announcements over the intercom at his junior high. He begins talking gibberish. 3. A priest is giving a sermon. A young girl in the back of the church screams.

Chapter Four

The Revision

The main rule of the writer is never to pity your manuscript.

–Isaac Bashevis Singer

You're not done yet!

You've only begun. When he was asked by the *Paris Review* if he revised, the Irish short story writer Frank O'Connor replied, "Endlessly, endlessly, endlessly." In fact, O'Connor rewrote many of his stories even after they were published. Ha Jin revises all his books at least thirty times. Ernest Hemingway told the *Paris Review* that he rewrote the end of *A Farewell to Arms*, the last page, thirty-nine times in order to "get the words right." Dorothy Parker said she couldn't write five words without revising seven. Good writing is rewriting. Bernard Malamud said it more eloquently: "The fruits of afterthought are sweet." Everyone writes. Writers rewrite. To err is human, to revise, divine.

Revision is not a matter of choice, so don't resist it. Now you have something to work with. A beginning, a middle, and an end. Now you have the opportunity and the responsibility to do justice to the lives of your characters. The first thing to do is put the draft away for as long as you can. Don't look at it. Write something else. Then go back to the draft with the fresh eyes and the objectivity that time provides. Reading your work well is a creative act. Read it out loud (if you can) and with a pen in your hand. Listen to your story. Take notes. What is the story trying to tell you? You cast a critical eye on your work. You see what you wrote, not what you thought you wrote. Writing a story is not supposed to be easy or quick or spontaneous. If it were, everyone would be doing it. And they're not. It's just us. As opera singer Beverly Sills once remarked, "There are no shortcuts to any place worth going."

Revision is where you become deeply engaged with your story, where you get to know your darlings so much better. This is not a time to polish—you still have a lot of smoothing to do. Revision is not the end of the creative process but a new beginning. Not just a chance to clean up but to open up and discover. In fact, you've been revising all along, revising as you wrote. Planning, drafting, and revising do not proceed in a linear fashion and are not even distinct tasks. They go on in draft one and draft twenty-one. Poet William Stafford thought that revision begins even before we write anything down. We might imagine that Melville opened *Moby-Dick*, which he was calling simply *The Whale*, like this:

~~My name is~~ Walter.
~~I go by~~ "Walter."
~~Folks~~ call me Walter.
Call me ~~Walter.~~
Call me Ishmael.

If you find yourself unenthusiastic, if you're putting off the revision process, ask yourself why. Perhaps you've written about characters you don't care about. Well, now's the time to get to know them—in writing, in your notebook. Find out the secrets that make them vulnerable and endearing and worth your time. Maybe you don't care who done it anymore. Maybe you didn't write about what is of crucial importance in your life. Why didn't you? Time to fix it here in draft two. If you don't want to do all this heavy lifting, if you don't look forward to the heavy lifting, then that's fine, but don't kid yourself, you are not now and will not be a fiction writer. Find another line of work or art. Writing fiction must be a labor of love, but it's also a love of labor.

Don't confuse revising with editing. To revise is to look again at your work with the intention of making a new and improved version of the story you're beginning to tell. While all editing is revision, not all revision is editing. Before you even think about edits and polish, you will read this draft that you thought was pretty damn fine already, and you'll reorganize material, examine words, phrases, and paragraphs, consider character, plot, and setting, look at your beginning, middle, and end. You'll add, shape, and delete. There are a thousand steps in the revision process. You'll uncover inconsistent characters, no doubt, a sputtering plot, rambling dialogue, flaccid verbs, insipid adjectives, unnecessary and intrusive adverbs, discordant prose, unwritten obligatory scenes, wavering tone, prosaic themes, an anemic sense of place. And so it goes. Your job is to remain cool and confident. You'll sort this out—by degrees. You'll make sense of the chaos—but not all at once and not just yet. You have achieved the state that John Keats called "negative capability"—or you had better do so soon. Negative capability, Keats defined as ". . . when a man is capable of being in uncertainties, mysteries, and doubts, without any irritable reaching after fact and reason." Stay calm and write on!

You may rearrange the plot by moving scenes and chapters. You may realize that one character has failed the audition and you'll have to let him go, but that another character has potential you haven't exploited yet. You'll take advantage of opportunities you gave yourself that you missed the first time through. You'll make sure that your scenes are set. You'll intensify the conflict and ramp up the tension. You make certain that while you may appear to digress, you do not actually digress. Anything more to be said about your themes? Are your images as vivid and significant as they can be?

You read the draft and ask the questions:

+ Have I shown and not told?

+ Is every scene essential?

+ Have I written the obligatory scenes?

+ Have I chosen the POV most likely to add interest and afford the reader the best access to the conflict?

+ Is the plot a causal sequence of events?

+ Has my central character changed? If so, how?

+ Have I made it hard enough for my central character?

+ Is the setting evocative?

+ Are the characters credible?

+ Does each character have a distinctive voice?

+ Have I started too early? Ended too late?

+ Is the material important?

+ Have I let my characters off the emotional hook?

+ Have I made the reader care about my people?

And the questions go on. You answer them honestly and get back to work. Make the needed changes. And start the whole process over again. And ask more questions:

+ What is my story about?

+ Was that my intention?

+ What emotional experience did I want my reader to have, and have I made that happen?

+ Is the story as clear as it can be?

Take your time—you can't do it all at once. Plot today, words tomorrow, characters on Thursday.

And for the moment, with the rewriting done for now, perhaps, you're ready for a **line edit**. Like revision, editing and proofreading are not optional. They're all part of the job. So you read the draft again with a pen in your hand. You keep in mind logic, clarity, and efficiency. In the line edit you'll address the creative content of your newly revised and improved draft. You examine your style and language at the sentence level. You're not looking for errors. You're determining if your prose is clear, fluid, fluent, and entertaining, if the tone is consistent, if the transitions are logical, if the language is as precise as you need it to be, or if it might be too abstract and general.

And then it's on to the **copy edit**. For this you'll want to have *The Chicago Manual of Style* on your desk and the unabridged *Merriam-Webster Dictionary* on your computer. In the copy edit you'll address the technical flaws in your manuscript. You'll read and review once again, this time to improve accuracy, to ensure that the text is free of grammar, usage, and mechanical errors, and free of inconsistencies. You want your manuscript to be accurate, clear, correct, and readable. So you'll fact-check and spell-check. You'll look for any sequential slip-ups, any lapses in logic

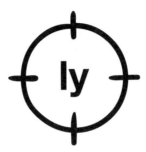

Here are some concerns you'll want to address in the copy-editing phase of revision. We'll start with **adverbs**. Stephen King wrote, "The road to hell is paved with adverbs." Gabriel García Márquez told his translator not to translate to English any adverbs ending in -*ly*, -*mente* in Spanish. Most of those -*ly* adverbs modify verbs. Annie Dillard said, "Adverbs are a sign that you've used the wrong verb." What you need are not two words, but one stronger word. Not, "He walked unsteadily," but "He staggered." So type *ly* into your search function on the computer and go to work. And here's some advice from Elmore Leonard: "Never use an adverb to modify the verb 'said' . . . he admonished gravely. To use an adverb this way (or almost any way) is a mortal sin. The writer is now exposing himself in earnest, using a word that distracts and can interrupt the rhythm of the exchange." Every adverb is an opportunity to think harder.

"Don't use **adjectives** that tell us how you want us to feel about the thing you are describing," C. S. Lewis wrote by way of advice to young writers. Like adverbs, adjectives can be intrusive—*the delightful gentleman*. Mark Twain wrote, "When you catch an adjective, kill it—perhaps the best advice for budding writers." Some adjectives are unnecessary. Often the adjectival concept is already in the noun modified. A night is dark, an ache painful, a needle sharp, a skyscraper tall. William Zinsser cites a practice he calls "adjective-by-habit." Not every cat is frisky, not every elm stately, not every detective hard-boiled, not every lagoon sleepy. So check all of your adjectives and be sure they are earning their keep. J. Anthony Lukas explained: "If the noun is good and the verb is strong, you almost never need an adjective."

Verbs are the rhetorical engines that drive your sentences that drive your story. Verbs move the characters who, in turn, move the reader. There are verbs of existence, condition, and action. You want your action verbs to be vivid, compelling, and propulsive. You want to make sure your verb is the precise verb. "It's precision that gives writing power," Gustave Flaubert wrote. Is your character *walking* or is he *parading, strolling, ambling, sauntering, stumbling, staggering, stepping, traipsing, schlepping, jaunting, pacing, hiking,* or *shuffling*? "Whatever you want to say," Flaubert told Maupassant, "there is only one word to express it, one verb to give it movement." And there's nothing so satisfying as coming upon an unexpected and accurate verb. Replace passive-voice verbs with active ones that are immediate, clear, and vigorous. "I kissed her" is better than "She was kissed by me." And it's shorter. On the other hand, you might choose the passive when the performer of the action is irrelevant: *My house was broken into last night.* Replace progressive forms of verbs with simple forms. "I stood guard" indicates a more definite time than "I was standing guard." And it's shorter. There are, of course, times when you want the progressive—to show actions taking place simultaneously: "I was standing guard when the walls were breached." With verbs of condition or existence—linking verbs—pay close attention to the verb "to be." We tend to overuse it. "To be" will be used (as it is here) as an auxiliary often enough. We're comfortable with it; it's flexible. But it's weak. Whenever you can, find a stronger, more assertive verb. Not "Yonder is your orphan with his gun," but "Yonder stands your orphan with his gun." Not "It was Dick who screamed," but "Dick screamed."

Nouns. Knowing the names of things can help you to see them. Knowing that this tree is not a generic palm but a princess palm helps you to see how it is different than that nearby Canary Island date palm. And your description will help the reader see the precise palm as well. In addition, knowing the names of things earns your narrator authority and credibility. You don't want your third-person narrator, for instance, to say that the dentist picked up that long, slim, silvery thing, you know—the what-do-you-call-it. And "He picked up the metal dental instrument," won't do, either. It could be a bone file or a spatula or a scaler. You can get visual dictionaries online and in print. If you are writing about a family's home you might want to know the difference between a bay window and an oculus window, between a cornice and a roof cresting, between a corner board and a drip edge.

What else? Maybe you don't really need that first paragraph of your story. Sometimes the first paragraph helps get the story going, but often it merely introduces the reader to the story you are about to tell. You may have had to write it, but we shouldn't have to read it. The action might actually begin in the second paragraph. So pick up the story and start reading with the second paragraph. And stop reading at your penultimate paragraph. Is that the real ending? If the last paragraph unnecessarily summarizes or explains the meaning of the story, cut it. And do you really need those exclamation points? If you find clichés or hackneyed words or phrases, cut them. Think harder. Whatever you're not sure of has to go. It doesn't belong. And now you can read the draft out loud. Listen for awkward and repetitious words, inadvertent rhyme, faulty rhythm. Your prose should be music.

And now you're ready to **proofread** for clarity, consistency, grammar, punctuation, spelling, and economy. This is your final pass, as it were, after you've done everything you can to make the story sing. Now you read to detect and correct errors and typos that slipped past you in the line and copy edits.

I have rewritten —often several times—every word I have ever published. My pencils outlast their erasers.

–Vladimir Nabokov

Editing & polishing, a checklist:

At the risk of being repetitive, we'll include this editing and polishing checklist. Let it serve as a gentle reminder and as a handy guideline.

1. Challenge every adverb
"The adverb is the enemy of the verb." Mark Twain said that. Or Unknown did—I've seen it attributed to both. Often what we need are not two words, one modifying, thus weakening, the other, but one stronger word. Not "She spoke loudly and persistently," but "She yammered." Adverbs modifying verbs of attribution are particularly intrusive and offensive. "'I see the problem,' she said confidently." Show us her confidence; don't tell us.

2. Challenge every adjective
"The adjective is the enemy of the noun," Voltaire said. (Hmm.) Mark Twain said, "As to the adjective: when in doubt, strike it out." Like adverbs, many adjectives are unnecessary. Color, for example, is often redundant, as in blue sky, green grass, and so on. Other adjectives are too conventional, like a tender heart or a sly fox.

3. Challenge every verb with an auxiliary
To reiterate: Replace passive-voice verbs with active ones. Replace progressive forms of verbs with simple forms. Use the progressive form only to show actions taking place simultaneously. (On the other hand, be sure to use the past perfect tense when denoting an action completed before a time in the past: "My mother had already called the plumber by the time I arrived." The calling took place before the arriving.)

4. Challenge the first paragraph
Sometimes the first paragraph helps get the story going, but often it merely introduces the reader to the story you are about to tell. Action might actually begin in the second paragraph. So pick up the story and start reading with the second paragraph.

5. Challenge the last paragraph
If the last paragraph unnecessarily summarizes or explains the meaning of the story, cut it out.

6. Challenge every line that you love

Dr. Johnson put it this way: "Read over your compositions, and whenever you meet with a passage which you think is particularly fine, strike it out." Distressing counsel, you might think. But the point is that you need to take out every word that is there for effect, every phrase you think is clever but is inessential, every sentence for which there is no purpose or point. Hemingway said prose is architecture, not interior decoration. Your concern must be with the characters and not with your own wit, style, or cleverness. If it's not advancing the plot, expressing the theme, or revealing the character, then it goes.

7. Challenge every exclamation point

Like adverbs, they are intrusive. You get, let's say, three exclamation points in your life. Use them wisely. Using an exclamation point is rather like laughing at your own joke.

8. Challenge every use of the verb "to be"

Again, whenever you can, find a more muscular and vigorous verb than the serviceable and anemic verb "to be."

9. Be alert for your pet words

They may be more pests than pets. They are the words you overuse without even knowing it. My own problem words are "very," "just," and "that." Delete them if they are not essential.

10. Be alert to your narrative weaknesses

Perhaps you tend to shift tenses for no reason or your first-person narrators tell too much and ignore the scenic. Know your tendencies and strengthen your writing by addressing them.

11. Be alert for every cliché

Or hackneyed word or phrase, every overused or unnecessary modifier. If you've heard it often, don't use it.

12. Cut every nonessential dialogue tag

In a conversation between two people, you may need only a single tag:

"Doris, I'm home," Lefty said.
"In the kitchen, dear. Did you remember the milk?"
"Got it right here."

And so on. The new paragraphs clearly indicate who is speaking.

13. Eliminate everything you're not sure of
If you doubt whether a sentence, word, or behavior belongs, it doesn't.

14. Read the draft aloud
Listen for awkward and repetitious words, inadvertent rhyme, faulty rhythm. Your prose should be music. Fiction needs to be at least as well written as poetry.

15. Proofread
For clarity, consistency, grammar, punctuation, spelling, economy. And then proofread again.

Look for verbs of muscle, adjectives of exactitude.

—Mary Oliver

Exercise 1:

Obsession

Reread your completed draft, and now you get to explore your brave new world. So describe one of your central character's obsessions, or something that haunts her, something you know about or you have an inkling of, but which does not yet appear in the story, or novel, at least not in black-and-white. Write about the obsession in as much detail as you can. (Maybe it's an obsession of your own—one you don't understand.) Now trace that obsession back to its source. Something happened in that character's childhood. You get an image, a person, an event. Write about that. (Your character is obsessed with security, with saving money, with playing it safe, because every payday Dad and Mom would fight about the family finances, frightening arguments for a five-year-old to witness.)

Exercise 2:

Insert Mode

For no reason at all, insert the following items (or one of them) into your story or novel: a recorded telephone message (one your character leaves or one he gets; from whom? a credit card company? Mom?); a menu (is she ordering out?); a portion of a radio talk show (NPR? Rush Limbaugh?); an original song (and here you get to write your own!). Now insert the following lines and continue with them. *This time last year I (or he/she) was . . . ; Five years from now I (he/she) will be . . . ; I (he/she) hear a knock at the door . . .* Some of these whacks on the narrative head might jar the story in a new and interesting direction. Try this. It's three in the morning and there's a knock at the door. Or the phone rings.

Exercise 3:

A Writer's Nightmare

Write about the most frightening and disturbing dream you've ever had. Or about a recurring dream. Or a confounding dream. Or the dream you had last night. Remember all of the details and write about the emotions you felt in the dream and feel now writing about it. Give that dream to your central character. And let's see what he makes of it.

Writing Every Day: Don't Break the Chain

Put a big "X" over every day you write something new (five minutes counts)!

Today, the first day of the rest of your writing life:

2	3	4	5	6	7	8	9	10	11	12	13	14
15	16	17	18	19	20	21	22	23	24	25	26	27
28	29	30	31	32	33	34	35	36	37	38	39	40
41	42	43	44	45	46	47	48	49	50	51	52	53
54	55	56	57	58	59	60	61	62	63	64	65	66
67	68	69	70	71	72	73	74	75	76	77	78	79
80	81	82	83	84	85	86	87	88	89	90	91	92
93	94	95	96	97	98	99	100	101	102	103	104	105
106	107	108	109	110	111	112	113	114	115	116	117	118
119	120	121	122	123	124	125	126	127	128	129	130	131
132	133	134	135	136	137	138	139	140	141	142	143	144
145	146	147	148	149	150	151	152	153	154	155	156	157
158	159	160	161	162	163	164	165	166	167	168	169	170
171	172	173	174	175	176	177	178	179	180	181	182	183
184	185	186	187	188	189	190	191	192	193	194	195	196
197	198	199	200	201	202	203	204	205	206	207	208	209
210	211	212	213	214	215	216	217	218	219	220	221	222
223	224	225	226	227	228	229	230	231	232	233	234	235
236	237	238	239	240	241	242	243	244	245	246	247	248
249	250	251	252	253	254	255	256	257	258	259	260	261
262	263	264	265	266	267	268	269	270	271	272	273	274
275	276	277	278	279	280	281	282	283	284	285	286	287
288	289	290	291	292	293	294	295	296	297	298	299	300
301	302	303	304	305	306	307	308	309	310	311	312	313
314	315	316	317	318	319	320	321	322	323	324	325	326
327	328	329	330	331	332	333	334	335	336	337	338	339
340	341	342	343	344	345	346	347	348	349	350	351	352
353	354	355	356	357	358	359	360	361	362	363	364	365

Leap year? Here's the extra day (a bonus): 366

Notes:

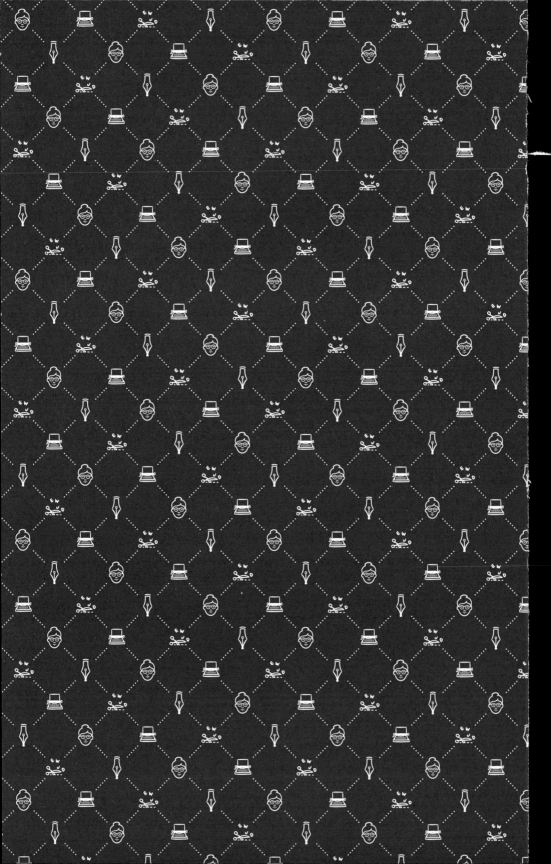